Oceans of Rum

The Nova Scotia Banana Fleet in Rum-Runner Heaven

David Mossman

Pottersfield Press, Lawrencetown Beach, Nova Scotia, Canada

Library and Archives Canada Cataloguing in Publication

Mossman, David J., author
Oceans of rum : the Nova Scotia banana fleet in rum-runner heaven / David Mossman.
ISBN 978-1-897426-76-0 (paperback)
1. Prohibition--Nova Scotia--History--20th century. 2. Smuggling--Nova Scotia--History--20th century. 3. Rum--Nova Scotia--History--20th century. 4. Nova Scotia--History--20th century. I. Title.
HV5091.C3M68 2016 364.1'336109716 C2015-907589-0

Cover design: Gail LeBlanc

We acknowledge the financial support of the Government of Canada through the Canada Book Fund for our publishing activities. We acknowledge the support of the Canada Council for the Arts. Nous remercions le Conseil des arts du Canada de son soutien. We are pleased to work in partnership with the Province of Nova Scotia to develop and promote our creative industries for the benefit of all Nova Scotians.

Pottersfield Press
83 Leslie Road
East Lawrencetown, Nova Scotia, Canada, B2Z 1P8
Website: www.PottersfieldPress.com
To order, phone 1-800-NIMBUS9 (1-800-646-2879) www.nimbus.ns.ca

Printed in Canada

Conseil des arts du Canada Canada Council for the Arts
Funded by the Government of Canada Financé par le gouvernement du Canada
Canada
NOVA SCOTIA

Dedicated to John (Jack) Ralph Spindler

We are no other than a moving row
Of Magic Shadow-shapes that come and go
Round with the Sun-illuminated Lantern held
In Midnight by the Master of the Show;

But helpless Pieces of the Game He plays
Upon this Chequer-board of Nights and Days;
Hither and thither moves, and checks, and slays,
And one by one back in the Closet lays.

– *Rubáiyát of Omar Khayyám*

Contents

Prologue	9
Introduction	11
Book 1 Setting the Scene	**15**
Like Father, Like Son	16
Evolution of Riverport and District	25
Race Day Tragedy	35
A Passing Way of Life	42
The Die is Cast: Mate Meets Future Commodore	48
Prohibition	54
Book 2 Rum-Running	**63**
Maritime Madness	64
Thou Shalt Not	72
The Banana Fleet	82
Al Capone's Namesake – Alpaca	91
"Say your prayers, boys!"	98
Playboy in Rum-Runner Heaven	110
Winter Run to Rum Row	115
Death in the Afternoon	118
Book 3 Sobering Up	**123**
The End of an Era	124
Cross Island Calamities	131
Laura	137
Matchmaking Soap Opera	144
Flashbacks	149
Crossing the Bar	162

Epilogue 166

Acknowledgements 169

Appendix 171

Works Consulted 173

Prologue

The rum-running era of the 1920s and 1930s cast long shadows across the history of Atlantic Canada. And Prohibition-era habits are evidently hard to shake. The numerous books on the subject invariably refer to the reticence of those most knowledgeable to speak their minds freely. Then there is the further problem of failing memory. In the words of Ainsley Fralick, fisheries inspector and former president of the Fisheries Museum of the Atlantic, "To tell the fact, I'm commencin' to dim." Thus is our history in danger of being lost.

After all, the captains hired by the fronts of shady syndicates behind rum-running operations were, in most instances, sworn to secrecy. My Uncle Teddy, Captain Winfred Spindler of Lower Rose Bay, Lunenburg County, Nova Scotia, was one of many individuals among the ranks of sea-going men in the province who chose to invest their time and talents in the rum trade. A surrogate father to me while I was growing up, he was in modern context a survivor. Adventuresome and resilient, he matured and endured through necessity, hard work, and tragedy, toward the end persevering like proverbial Job through his allotted ninety-three years.

Prohibition was immediately opposed by the efforts of wealthy American financiers and criminal organizations. An elite group of rum-runners efficiently ran a very profitable enterprise. Their ships were known as the Banana Fleet, because most of them had a profile modelled along the lines of a low-slung World War I submarine chaser. Almost all of them had Lunenburg County crews from Riverport.

The book you hold presents a portrait of a man, an era, and a community. It is, in a sense, a three-cornered chronicle involving Spindlers, Ritceys, and Romkeys – local surnames all – an account tinged with tragedy and intrigue. Illustrative of ordinary lives where little things can, and often do, turn out to mean a lot, the focus is on the Nova Scotia community of Riverport and District and the life of one man, a fisherman and former rum-runner sea captain, Winfred Oswald Spindler, the only son of John Solomon and Clara Augusta Spindler.

Growing up a deep-sea fisherman, the rough and ready rum-running years, which for Winfred lasted from 1923 to 1938, were memorable on many carefree counts: excitement, camaraderie, drama on the high seas, love affairs, big payoffs, and fast cars. However, tragedies lay in wait for him all along the way – unfair to sidestep in review, yet impossible to explain to anyone's satisfaction or even to mention dispassionately. During his years at sea, apart from shore fishing, he sailed on no less than twenty vessels, including rum-runners. Although he probably did not realize it, Winfred had charisma, even rigged out in oilskins, and it doubtless contributed to his popularity in the community. He was Spinny throughout Riverport and District, Winfred or Ted to his parents and sisters, Uncle Teddy or less commonly Teddy to most of his extended family, Skipper or Captain to his shipmates. Each of these names finds compelling place and time in this account, helping to define the man according to the occasion.

Introduction

October, 1934, Lower Rose Bay School

Marguerite Myra, an eighteen-year-old schoolteacher on probation for one term at the Lower Rose Bay School, considered lighting the stove near the back of the room, for the chill of mid-October was in the air. But she feared not being able to control the thing and, at the same time, all eight grades of students, once it got going. A homemade affair carved out of a 44-gallon oil drum, the stove had yielded disastrously smoky results on a previous occasion, so she decided against it. Could be her best efforts were being sabotaged by her young charges. She knew tricks were sometimes played on new teachers. Anyway, it was Friday, and she would ask someone's advice about the stove on the weekend. The room would heat up fast enough, she thought, as the children shuffled to their seats and her teaching day began.

That small single-storey one-room rural school served to introduce numerous local rustics, Winfred Spindler among them, to elementary aspects of the three Rs. As a young lad, he attended this school, a very short walk from his home, before gratefully graduating at age thirteen to sail on a salt-banker to the Grand Banks. By the fall of 1934, the worn spruce floorboards in the old building voiced their welcome to the mobs as they made their way, trudging to or fleeing from, confinement.

Outside, a flat patch of well-worn ground provided a small field for games, usually tag and the popular game of sticks. Thriftiness as a policy permeated all aspects of school activities, as it did in the wider community. This game did not even require a ball. Rocks served as goal posts, and an even number of sticks located on the ground beside each goal were the trophies. Roughhousing took place on the sidelines where patches of grass supplied welcome arenas for clumps of wrestling boys, locations carefully avoided by girls. Levelling the playing field, just behind the school, a two-seater outhouse awaited customers, though its upkeep – in common with its kind elsewhere – generally left much to be desired by modern standards.

When mid-morning recess was declared, most of the children made their customary quick exit to the playground. It was one of those magically calm days in the fall. There was no wind, and the harbour waters showed scarcely a ripple. Several small groups commenced games in the schoolyard. But quite a number of these born and bred beachcombers made their way across the public road to where a rising tide lapped ever so gently along the slate-lined shore. No telling what you might discover there.

This morning, the excitement level in the schoolyard seemed excessive. Fearing a possible crisis, Marguerite looked out of the window and down toward the shore. The schoolyard was quickly emptying. The children were shouting to each other and running pell-mell down to the shore. There, beside an old fish shed, she beheld an exuberant group frantically digging in a bed of dry sea grass. Even as she looked on in astonishment, the sea grass flew and (good heavens!) children were taking off in all directions, a bottle held tightly in each hand. Before long there was not a child in sight.

The ringing bell signalling the end of recess yielded no young faces, eager or otherwise. The fact is the children were busy putting to work what they learned at home. They were all familiar with the practice of hiding rum beneath floorboards and basement stairs, in flour barrels and in secret closets, in the woods, in woodpiles, in barns, and in hidey holes along the shores of this hot-spot community of rum-runners. Kids are ever ready to play pirate. Finders keepers, losers weepers! They did not concern themselves with the question of whether the evil of society caused the rum-running (smuggling), or whether the do-gooders were to blame. But they knew all about the drop-offs being made at coves and crannies along the extensive coastline throughout Riverport and District. And they were well warned about repeating what was said around the dinner table.

Later that afternoon, little bums turned up to polish the already well-shined schoolroom seats. No questions were asked, and no explanations offered as the children trickled in. They were unusually quiet and avoided eye contact. And Marguerite, finding herself on unfamiliar ground, did not question. She was in unknown territory. The beneficiaries of the free liquor from the schoolhouse heist were certainly not going to talk, and whoever failed to take delivery of a contracted cache was effectively muzzled.

Winfred Spindler on the deck of the replica of the tall ship *Bounty*, built in Lunenburg in 1960 for the movie *Muntiny on the Bounty*, released in 1962.

Book 1
Setting the Scene

Like Father, Like Son

Inside every older person is a younger person wondering what the hell happened.

– Cora Harvey Armstrong

Winfred Oswald Spindler was born of Clara Augusta and Captain John Solomon Spindler in their old Cape Cod house in Lower Rose Bay on October 8, 1899. Winfred was a sixth-generation Nova Scotian of undiluted Foreign Protestant[1] stock, and the Atlantic Ocean laps the doorstep of his ancestral home. Like most boys of his vintage, it was not long before he learned the practical side of the fishing business. Sons were expected to help fathers. Thus the art and practice of shore fishing with his father was part of the natural progression of things.

But given a clear day, from the homes in Rose Bay the great clouds of white canvas on Grand Banks schooners sailing in the distance to and from Lunenburg exerted a tremendous attraction on youthful imaginations. Daily life in this patriarchal community was a sort of tribal affair, a well-practised ritual understood by everyone.

1 Foreign Protestants were prospective settlers of Swiss, German, and French origin, dispatched from 1750-1752 by the British Lords of Trade to counterbalance the French and their Catholic presence in Nova Scotia.

On the shore below the Spindler homestead in Lower Rose Bay in late summer, ca. 1910, John Solomon Spindler (centre) and Benjamin Cook show off a large cod just about the size of young Teeman Zinck and an unidentified girl.

After getting the basics, young Winfred shunned the country school a short distance away, leaving experiments in higher education to his sisters Helen Viola (my mother) and Emily Drusilla. He opted instead to attend a school of hard knocks. He knew everyone in his village, and pretty well everyone knew him. If they were unsure of the young fellow's identity, he'd hear the familiar refrain "Aren't you John Solomon's boy?"

Like other fishermen, John Solomon and his son also fished lobsters in season, a portion of the catch feeding into a cannery located in Upper Rose Bay on the shore near Burnt Corner north of Conrads Island. John Solomon served as foreman at the factory. As Alistair MacLeod describes in his short story "Vision", "Lobster factories were set up along the coast for the canning of the lobsters at a time before good land transportation and refrigeration became common. In May and June and into July the girls in white caps and smocks packed the lobster meat into burnished cans before they were steam sealed." Delivered live to the factory, the shellfish fetched three cents for small, and seventeen cents for large lobsters.[1]

Family archives and records conserved by Maxwell Lohnes in *Captains of Lunenburg County* and compiled for the Fisheries Museum of the Atlantic show that John Solomon was master of the two-masted schooner *Blanche,* a sailing vessel 37 feet in length, 13 feet in breadth, 4 feet in depth, and gross tonnage 12 tons. It was probably a "Tancook whaler," double-ended with a clipper bow and centreboard. His favourite fishing ground was the prolific Western Banks, an area nearly as large as Cape Breton extending over one hundred kilometres west-southwest from the western end of Sable Island. About 160 kilometres from Lunenburg, it was noted in those days for its cod, haddock, and halibut and entailed a trip lasting a day or more from Riverport. Made in company, usually with one or two crew members and on occasion his son Winfred, those trips were rather more risky and rigorous than inshore fishing. This was good experience for young Winfred and, showing an independent spirit and love of adventure, he signed Ship's Articles[2] on a Grand Banks schooner.

In 1912, at the age of thirteen, he graduated from flunky to header on *Revenue,* a schooner captained by John Zinck. The job – cutting the heads off the daily catch of cod fish, some of which weighed twenty-five pounds or more – earned him the princely sum of $1.50 per month. However, it was not long before his promotion to doryman. All told, Winfred spent over ten years working (as deckhand, doryman, or mate) shoulder to shoulder with other sailors in the perilous business of manning Grand Banks schooners.

I learned a great deal from my father and my uncle about life as a Grand Banks fisherman. And the sea remained a big draw for young wharf rats even in the very last days of schooner fishing. My

---

1 The factory in Upper Rose Bay was one of 142 in Nova Scotia in 1924. In 1920, the first year lobster fishing licenses were required, the factories in the Maritime Provinces packed tails and claws into one-pound cans to the tune of 160,000 cases (48 cans to the case).

2 Ship's Articles: the contract by which the sailor agrees to the conditions, pay rate, etc., for the ship they are going to work.

mother made very sure not to encourage me. An academic, she had other plans for her children. But my father made blue water sailing a lifelong pursuit. He stuck with it right up to the mid-1950s. And he was quick enough to encourage me when I showed a brief spark of interest following the spring trip in 1952.

"You could come along as flunky, if you like," he offered.

But it's one of those things that I'll forever, sort of, regret. As the saying goes, You can never go back. I opted instead for inshore fishing that summer with my uncle.

After coming in from fishing, and a much-needed midday dinner, Uncle Teddy and I used his battered old splitting table for processing the catch. While he did most of the heavy lifting, on a daily basis I combined the roles of throater, straight-edged knife sharpener, and general gofer flunky. Together we processed – deboned, cleaned, and washed – the catch of mostly cod, ready for salting down in a puncheon kept in his nearby shingled grey fish shed.

Like all good flunkies, I extracted the cod tongues for family consumption or for sale in the community. Proof is manifest by several knife scars on the index finger of my left hand. The obstinate shore upon which these accidents took place is still there too, but only a small heap of rotting boards and some lonely ancient panes of glass left staring at the sky mark the location of that shabby fish shed and many fond memories. Decades later, yet familiar as breathing, I see us sharing good times while shore fishing and fair weather sailing. The storyline was likely more scripted and rigorous on a salt-banker.

"On the Banks years ago," Uncle Teddy says, as we work away down on the shore, "on a good trip, there'd be as many as four splitting tables set up on deck. We'd be up sometimes 'til midnight, two to three days in a row. We didn't do a whole lot of sleepin'. In the mornings, anywhere between two and three o'clock, comes the call, 'Turn out, all hands on deck!' Settin' up flare pots of kerosene light on the galley house and the dories, we'd bait up our trawls, and before long we'd be away."

On the rolling deck of the *Irene Mary*, fishermen struggle with a large haul of cod. Two splitting tables are in view here; two others are behind the photographer. Dories hang each side ready for launching; the vertical pipe (front right) is a silencer for the diesel engine, many of which were installed in schooners in the 1920s. (Photograph from Elwood Geldert's *Farewell Old Salts*, with permission of The Fisheries Museum of the Atlantic)

"Before breakfast?" I ask incredulously.

"Yes, we'd set out our trawl first thing, and then come back for breakfast."

Don't know that I could handle that, I'm thinking to myself. No two ways about it, salt-banking was a hard life; long exhausting hours, in constant danger of being run over, or into, during the night or in a fog, or of being washed overboard in shipwreck or storms. Less spectacular accidents were common, though they scarcely qualified as news to fishermen very long after the event. Even a simple trip to the toilet might prove a perilous pursuit. My uncle describes one such occasion experienced by his next-door neighbour and one-time shipmate, Leo Zinck, early one day on the Banks.

"You know," Uncle Teddy says, "it's difficult to do even a number one while at work in a dory at sea. Some men who have tried it haven't survived it – falling overboard, and most of 'em

Fresh fishing in the winter. The "spot buoy" is the wooden barrel in the rigging on the right side, ready to mark their fishing spot when they go to port after ten days to land their catch. Note the lights strung for dressing fish at night. (Photograph courtesy of John Kingwell)

not knowing how to swim, they sink pretty quickly. Boots fill, and heavy clothes drag a man down. And it's just about impossible to do a number two – except in your pants. Anyway, there was this time Leo and his dory mate, they finished their first set, and got back on board ship. It was blowin' a fair breeze and a sea was getting up. But before breakfast, Leo, there was no way he could wait any longer. He had to go bad, so he took the draw bucket and made a beeline for the head."

"What do you mean, draw bucket?" I interrupt.

"You know what I mean by the head[1]?" he asks then, to which I nod in reply.

---

1 The head was the toilet used by sailors. It was located at the very head or bow of the ship, necessarily downwind, and accessible to wave action (for flushing) if fixed in an open box-shaped arrangement next to the bowsprit on the earliest schooners. In the twentieth-century schooners, a galvanized bucket on a rope served the purpose. The captain had a separate hand-operated toilet in the stern gallery.

"Well," he continues, "you use what we call the draw bucket – a galvanized bucket with a rope tied to the handle – for drawing up water from over the side. If it's fine, a man does his business at the head, that is, between the nested dories. If it's really foul weather, he'll go into one of the top dories and use the bucket there. Bucket and chuck it, is how it works, you see. Anyways, somehow or other in the process, Leo lost his footing as the ship rolled, and over he went. Somebody raised a cry, and we lined the rails, but could see no sign of him. Seems we slowly run right over him. The ship was practically lying-to at the time, so what happened was, he must have got bumped slowly along the whole length of the keel. Then, right at the stern we caught sight of yellow oilskins near enough to the surface to try an' snag him with a gaff. And that we managed to do. He was some lucky. But it took us quite a while for to bring him around."

Although their role as food providers exempted Winfred and his shipmates from call-up during World War I, they experienced close calls at sea. Apart from natural hazards, schooner captains were often obliged to take evasive measures to escape the predations of German U-boats tasked with disrupting the offshore fisheries, as well as cargo and troop shipments. Winfred recalls that late on the afternoon of Friday, August 30, 1918, aboard the *Frances W. Smith* sailing out of Lunenburg with Captain Forman Mossman, a steamer came out to warn the schooners. Most ships left their trawls un-hauled and made for port as quickly as possible. But Captain Mossman ordered his crew to haul theirs before heading for home. They were fortunate to escape penalty.

But nearby, Captain Irvin Eisenhauer of the *Elsie Porter* was suddenly confronted by U-boat 117, which broke water ominously beside the stationary schooner. He was ordered aboard the U-boat to meet the captain, who treated him civilly and gave him a drink. Irvin said he held his glass high and proposed a toast: "Peace all over the world." To which Kapitan Otto Dröscher[1] replied, "Pieces before peace." The *Elsie Porter* was sunk with bombs and returned its cargo of one thousand quintals of fish to the sea, as her crew began the 470-kilometre row to Newfoundland.

Some vessels put in to Port Hawkesbury before proceeding further along the coast, while others headed directly to Lunenburg, hugging the coast as closely as they dared. Towards evening, high winds surprised the *Frances W. Smith*, taking out her jib then blowing away the foresail. By storm's end, so Winfred said, she had her skylight beaten in and every last dory destroyed.

Immediately following the Great War, freight rates on lumber to the West Indies remained high. The war exacted a huge toll on steel steamships, so consequently schooners were in great demand. According to John Parker in *Sails of the Maritimes*, "the year 1919 saw the largest number of big wooden schooners launched in Atlantic Canada." After fishing was over in 1918, Winfred signed on as a crew member aboard the schooner *Harold Conrad*, captained by George Backman, freighting lumber down south. During the trip, Winfred had a memorable dispute with a Spanish-speaking stevedore in Trinidad.

That Trinidad business, that was pretty close for me, I think. That time we went down with a load of lumber from Liverpool. The deck load was for Bermuda, and the lumber in the hold was for Trinidad. We did some rolling with that sort of cargo.

Anyway, we left and went down, bound for Bermuda and Trinidad. Had a good trip down to Bermuda, landed, and took the deck load off. Then on to Trinidad, six or seven hundred miles further south, near the equator, about ten degrees from the equator. So, it's hot as the dickens. And we got there, and in the hold it must have been a lot over one hundred [degrees], and I said to one of the crew, "I'm not going to work in this heat for only twenty dollars a month."

---

1 From August 10 to November 9, 1918, Dröscher's U-boat sank 20 ships and damaged four others along the eastern Atlantic seaboard. He surrended his ship and crew to the Americans on November 21, 1918.

Anyways, we was there, and I said to a Spaniard, "Could I hire you to take out cargo in my place?" Yes, he said. "And how much do you want?" I wanted to save some money for rum. He said two dollars. I said OK. That wasn't much, but it was a lot out there in Trinidad. I'd have given him some more money if I'd have had it.

So that was all right, only they didn't take out cargo that afternoon. They didn't work. I don't know what happened. And when the time came to give up work, around about four or five o'clock, he hadn't worked at all. And along he came for his money. "Money?" I said. "Why? You didn't work." He kind of insisted, but I didn't want to part with two dollars. I could have bought a couple of bottles of rum with that. Anyway, that was all right. I went ashore that evening, three of us. And as soon as we got on the wharf, I saw these three Spaniards there, three young fellows.

So we started uptown. And we saw them keep following us. So I say to them, "Run along. What do you want?" And the fellow says, "I want my money." And I say, "I don't owe you any money." So we kept walking along. Then one of my shipmates says to me, "That man has a knife in his hand." Then I started to think it over, and what to do.

And we went along a little ways, and there was a cop there and he could speak some English. So I explained to him that there wasn't all that much involved, not a hundred dollars. Well, he didn't say I had to pay the two dollars, but he told me, "I advise you to pay him, and it might save you a lot of trouble." Well, if he'd have run up and stabbed me in the back that wouldn't have been so good – out in Trinidad, somewhere in hospital. So imagine how that would have been. Anyway, after I gave him the two dollars, away he went, and that was the last I saw of the Spaniard.

Evolution of Riverport and District

Everything changes and nothing stands still.
– Heraclitus of Ephesus (ca. 535-475 BCE)

Champlain's 1604 map of the Port de La Hève shows aboriginal settlements on the eastern side of the La Hève River near present-day Riverport. These were the teepees and longhouses of their traditional summer encampments. By 1632, the first permanent French settlement was in place, governed by Isaac de Razilly, delegated by King Louis XIII as Lieutenant-General and Viceroy of New France. Historic records show that a good relationship existed between the indigenous peoples and the early French settlers. The settlers moved freely on both sides of the river, although their habitations clustered around Fort Sainte Marie-de-Grâce on the west side. However, an entrepreneur, Nicolas Denys, who accompanied de Razilly in 1632, built on the east side of the river and started a lumber business and an inshore fishery.

During French occupation, the name La Hève applied to the entire area on both sides of the river. On Bellin's 1744 map, L'Anse aux Huitres was the name given to what in the 1880s would become Ritcey's Cove. But this was long after the French shelved interest in the area in favour of a settlement at Port Royal. The indigenous peoples, familiar with the region now for thousands of years, were Mi'kmaq, one among a cluster of Eastern Algonquin tribes. In their nomadic communities, leadership was reportedly based not on power but prestige and the ability to successfully manage the hunting and fishing. In consequence, their way of life was adversely affected by European activities, not least as their trade advantages disappeared and various military alliances were attempted. Early depopulation and sociocultural disruptions took a severe toll on the Mi'kmaq as a distinctive people. Their traditional right to roam was increasingly restricted. By the early 1950s, a forced relocation scheme taken from the same book as the concept of residential schools went the distance to completing their social isolation.

Up until the early 1940s, the Mi'kmaq commonly made temporary summer encampments along the Nova Scotia coast. Fisherfolk in Rose Bay were familiar with some of these. Locations favoured by the Mi'kmaq for gathering alders and dyes for basket making included one along the shore close by the lobster factory in Upper Rose Bay. Another was on the north shore of Rose Head near Rocker Cove. Gypsies too, in their white covered wagons, paid occasional visits to the community. As Maude Bortner reminisces in *Bits and Pieces of the Way it Was,* "The Indians, when they came, made baskets, but the gypsies made tinware something like the 'tinkers' in England who travelled the country roads selling their wares during the summer."

Major change took place in the middle of the eighteenth century with the arrival of the Foreign Protestant pioneer Johann Phillipp Henericie, founding member of a new settlement. Born in Germany in 1731, and following transport to the New World and marriage to Anna Catarina in 1751, he set to work building a log cabin on the Riverport shore in 1754. By the 1880s, and following Henericie's name change to Ritcey, the place became known as Ritcey's Cove, taking its name from the eastern bay of the LaHave River estuary where his ancestors first landed. Then, in 1902, the town's citizens met to decide between the names Fairhaven and

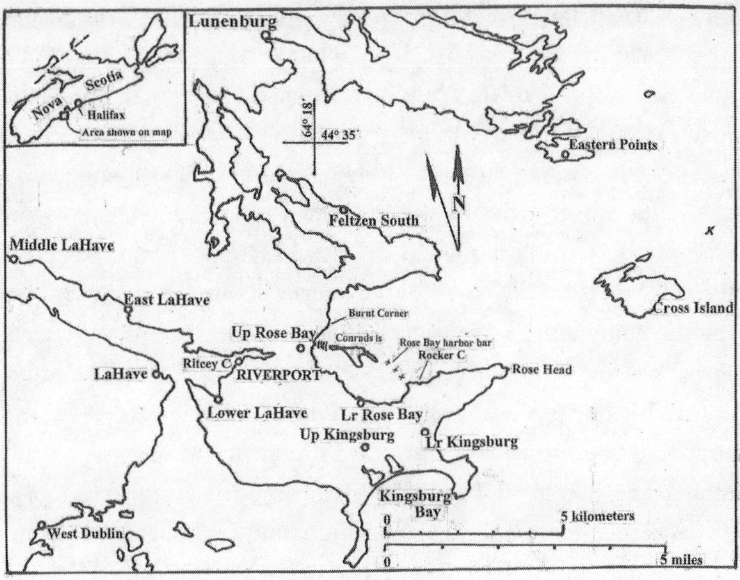

A map showing the extent of Riverport and District reveals it as a ragged peninsula thrust into the Atlantic.

Riverport. The tie-breaking vote was cast in favour of Riverport by the meeting's chairman, Simon Ritcey, a direct descendent of Johann.

Already by the late 1750s the Foreign Protestants had begun taking over LaHave. Today, Riverport and District includes the communities of Riverport, Lower LaHave, East LaHave and Middle LaHave, Upper and Lower Rose Bay, Upper and Lower Kingsburg, Bayport, and Feltzen South. A typical extended Nova Scotia tribal village, one might suppose.

In the beginning, the Methodists, which formed the largest religious denomination in the district, travelled from Ritcey's Cove to Lunenburg for worship. History acknowledges the congregation as part of the Lunenburg Circuit in 1825. By 1843 or 1844, they erected a small church on the waterfront in the village of Riverport where Ritcey Brothers store now stands. Then, late in 1870, a new church was completed in Upper Rose Bay to service the wider community. A major addition in 1897 allowed for accommodation of 650, and on June 10, 1925, the church – Trinity United – became part of the United Church of Canada. Close to slingshot distance from each other, it keeps company with the Presbyterian and the Lutheran churches, each with its own magnificent pipe organ.

A four-room school was constructed in 1905 in Riverport and three teachers were appointed to instruct from primary to grade eleven in three of the rooms; the fourth served as the office. By now the community was thriving. It even had its own weekly newspaper, *The Riverport Times*. In 1915, Charles and Saint Clair Ritcey formed Ritcey Brothers Ltd., and in 1917 incorporated it for the purpose of outfitting and operating the vessels necessary for salt fishing. The Riverport Telephone Company was organized in 1893 to provide service throughout the community, although dial phones did not come in until 1938. The Riverport Electric Light Commission, the oldest independent facility of its kind in the province, was established in 1920. That same year, Samuel Ritcey's general store was re-established – 166 years after Henericie's arrival in the New World – called Ritcey and Creaser after Russell Ritcey and his business partner Robie Creaser.

The captain and crew members were major shareholders in the salt-bankers operated from Riverport, with Ritcey Brothers doing the managing and outfitting. During the Depression of the late 1920s and early 1930s, the Riverport fishing fleet diminished to one schooner, the *Mavis Barbara*. Only the guarantees to suppliers by some minor shareholders saved the company from going under. The herring processing business, developed in the late 1930s, also helped maintain the viability of the company. However, major changes were in the works, thanks to an infusion of funds generated by the rum-running era. As we shall see, this came about in large measure through the efforts of fisherman and rum-runner turned businessman Willoughby R. Ritcey, another chip off the old Henericie block.

Lacking formal education (like most of his boyhood friends),

Willoughby's sea-going career was rudely interrupted when his foot was mangled by a deck engine. His father, Captain Egerton Ritcey, with whom he sailed, greatly lamented having bought his boy the hip rubber boots that were caught up in the flywheel, causing the accident. Sensing opportunity during the early years of rum-running, the young man turned entrepreneur. Fitted with a wooden leg, Willoughby made the best of a bad deal by adapting to life ashore. And although wooden legs among seamen are the stuff of legend, Willoughby would make local legend as a dry-land prince of rum-running rather than clumping about on a vessel's rolling deck. It seems he possessed a very keen mind for business.

W.R., the moniker by which everyone in Riverport and District – and many well-connected individuals far beyond – knew him, always enjoyed a good time. This particular trait made a convenient fit for his chosen career. It is said that his artificial appendage was used to advantage on party occasions when W.R. impressed the ladies by plunging a knife into his wooden leg to make a point.[1] Hometown boy makes good, despite the pain.

In 1943, the rich and highly respected W.R. bought into Ritcey Brothers and incorporated a subsidiary company, Ritcey Brothers Fisheries Ltd. Under his direction Ritcey Brothers Ltd. became exporters of salt fish, and to speed things up, the subsidiary acquired a fleet of vessels. Stanley Nauss, an ex-Bank of Montreal employee, continued to oversee all of W.R.'s business operations. The fish-drying plants in Riverport and nearby Kraut Point, which also had a cold storage facility, were kept busy. As W.R. freely admitted, although the rum-running business had been good, the fishing business was even better.

As captain of several rum-runners, my uncle had close dealings with W.R. during the 1930s, but when World War II broke out, he went back to shore fishing. Otherwise, many of the old cliques

1 Proof of this practice may be preserved on one or more of W.R.'s wooden legs, which somehow found their way into the Fisheries Museum of the Atlantic and are currently archived in the eaves.

formed around W.R. during rum-running held fast. A close colleague from the very beginning, Captain Byron Ritcey, became foreman at the plant at Kraut Point. Other former rum-runners served as W.R.'s schooner captains. For example, Joey Wentzell skippered the *Sally Irene* which, at 149 feet long (compared with the 143-foot-long *Bluenose*), was one of the largest ships built for Ritcey Brothers Fisheries. We shall learn more about these individuals later. Suffice to say that W.R. was intimately involved in the careers of numerous mariners – rum-runners and otherwise – who crewed vessels sailing out of Riverport.

By 1950, one of W.R.'s companies, Riverport Shipping, had a salt-fishing fleet of twelve-dory schooners including the *E.F. Zwicker, Judith Irene, Sally Irene, Jean Frances, Pasadena II, Irene Mary,* and the *Arthur J. Lynn.* He also had an old English-built freighter, the *Clyde Valley,* which did yeoman service transporting salt fish to the Caribbean and on occasion returning with consignments of liquor. I am advised that at least the largest portion of this cargo usually reached its official destination, the Nova Scotia Liquor Commission. W.R.'s salt fish plant was one of the largest in Canada, and in a peak season handled over fifteen million pounds of salt fish. These were halcyon days in this modest Maritime community.

The image is sharply fixed in my memory: my father at home in Rose Bay in 1950, pointing out Willoughby Ritcey (no direct relation to Russell) driving by in his big shiny new Buick. Everyone, but everyone, knew and respected the wealthy and community-minded W.R., the undisputed king of the community. Many families owed their income to his enterprises, all of which prospered during rum-running, and thereafter for several decades working on fishing ships and facilities which he established and sustained. He was generous too in helping fund the higher education of deserving students in the community. To keep his businesses busy and running smoothly, W.R. had his own carpenters, plumbers, electricians, and painters, whose services he generously made available to homeowners in the community.

Launch of Ritcey Brothers Fisheries Ltd. schooner *Irene Mary* in Smith and Rhuland's Shipyards, Lunenburg. (Photograph by Gilbert Kempton)

My father sailed on the *Clyde Valley* and on some of W.R.'s schooners, and I was among several young "herring chokers" who landed their very first paying jobs working in W.R.'s herring processing plant on Ritcey's Wharf in Riverport. At thirty-five cents an hour, we stood clothed in oilskins towards the end of the line, each of us striplings with a big brush in hand, scrubbing the gut-linings clean of blood and gurry (fish offal) on a few thousand herring each day. To us, that was good money, although I much preferred shore fishing with my uncle who, at this time, had little direct interaction with W.R. As we shall see, however, quite a different relationship held between the two men during the last several years of rum-running.

Regular shipments of salt fish went from Riverport to the New York market, and to Greece, Italy, Brazil, and Chile, and in the Caribbean to Cuba, Haiti, the Dominican Republic, Puerto Rico, Trinidad, and British Guiana (now Guyana). However, by far the largest market was Cuba. Unfortunately, the takeover of Cuba by Fidel Castro in 1959 disrupted the market severely because all sales were in U.S. dollars and these were no longer available to that nation. Consequently, and coincident with the sudden growth of the fresh fish industry, the decline of the salt fish industry occurred.

Under W.R.'s direction, Ritcey Brothers Fisheries turned to operating a fleet of longliners and scallop draggers to access the growing fresh fish markets. The longliners were developed from the Cape Island boats (originally designed on Cape Sable Island), but were up to sixty feet long, heavier built and capable of a greater range and a far longer season. Operating a trawl set through a chute over the stern, they presaged still larger and more efficient trawlers and draggers. His several scallop draggers were so-called wet fish trawlers, dragging from the stern and returning to port with their cargo of scallops in shells. These would then be shucked by special working crews based on shore, each dragger yielding on average 10,000 to 20,000 pounds of scallops.

In 1965, W.R. oversaw the sale of Ritcey Brothers Fisheries to H.B. Nickerson Ltd., who converted it into a modern fresh fish processing plant, Riverport Seafoods, located at Kraut Point. In the meantime, the schooners *Irene Mary, Sally Irene,* and *Pasadena II* were lost at sea; the *E.F. Zwicker* and *Arthur J. Lynn* were sold to the U.S. International Seaman's Union as training vessels; the *Jean Frances* was sold into freighting to a Halifax company; and the *Judith Irene* was converted to a scallop boat, the new fish of choice on which the industry swiftly focused. And, although Ritcey and Creaser was sold to D.W. Craig Enterprises in 1968, Ritcey and Creaser, as well as Ritcey Brothers, remain household words in the community even today.

Time was marching on. The king passed away on August 10, 1969. Following W.R.'s death, relatively prosperous times endured until September 27, 1981, when a major fire destroyed the processing plant and the main building, which housed the shipping records, and the government wharf at Kraut Point. Over six hundred workers suddenly found themselves bereft of income.

And although a concrete wharf was built in 1983, it has seen little commercial activity except for that of *Atlantic Destiny*,[1] a giant freezer scallop dragger which sails out of Kraut Point for Ocean Choice International, a company based in Newfoundland. Several similar ships sailing out of Shelburne, and one out of LaHave, account for most of the allowable scallop quota. Average catch for one trip ranges between 150,000 and 160,000 pounds of scallops.

Destiny indeed! Applied to the spectrum of possibilities, the word conjures up an immediate puzzle. Does anyone know what the future holds? You can wonder all you want about it without achieving anything, least of all disposing of further speculation. A case in point concerns the future of Riverport and District. And within that community, the destiny of Winfred Spindler continued to unfold, unpredictably, in what for him will have been a particularly formative experience.

---

1 Routinely, *Atlantic Destiny* fishes for twenty days on Georges Bank catching and processing scallops. Three rakes, one each side and one at the stern, catch the shellfish which are then machine-shucked of their shells. Except for the muscles ("meats" of the fish), shells and flesh are discarded at sea. Returning to its shore base, the ship unloads the frozen scallops, takes on a fresh crew, and leaves for the fishing ground on the very same day.

Winfred Spindler at 21 in 1920.

Race Day Tragedy

Half-mast high the signal floats!
She's coming in from sea;
Some sailor of her crew is gone –
Who may the lost one be?

– Author unknown

Winfred no sooner arrived in Riverport after the fall fishing trip on the *Mary Pauline* with Captain Dan Romkey in 1920 than he received a welcome invitation. It came from his childhood friend Calvin (Cal) Lohnes, captain of the knockabout schooner (no bowsprit) *Ruby L. Pentz,* who wanted Winfred to round out his crew for a big racing event. Everyone had heard about the first North Atlantic Fisherman's International Race, a race series established by the *Halifax Herald* newspaper. The prize at stake was better known as the International Fisherman's Trophy, and the race between the U.S. and Canadian fishing schooners was scheduled to be held in early October off the coast of Halifax. Was Winfred interested in signing on? The question was a no-brainer for Winfred. There was nothing he loved more than the thrill of being on a schooner running free, seas plunging over the bow, wind howling in the rigging, and the sight of canvas strained to the limit.

The Grand Banks schooner *Ruby L. Pentz* arrives on October 8, 1920, in Halifax harbour to participate in the elimination race among Canadian schooners to determine which one would compete against the Americans in the first North Atlantic Fisherman's International Race – won later that year by the American entry *Esperanto*. (Photo by Commercial Photo Service. From the W.R. MacAskill Collection, no. 244, Nova Scotia Archives)

The race for the International Fisherman's Trophy would be held between real working schooners. First on the program was the elimination race to determine which Canadian schooner would compete against the American entry. On October 11, 1920, that race saw the *Ruby L. Pentz* (the only LaHave schooner to take part in the race) finish seventh out of a field of a dozen or more entries. *Delawana,* skippered by Tommy Himmelman, beat out Angus Walters, whose *Gilbert B. Walters* lost her topmast during the last leg of the race. Alas, a week later *Delawana* was roundly defeated by the Gloucester, Massachussetts, entry, *Esperanto*. That outcome spurred the building (in six months!) of the *Bluenose.* The rest is some of the best of Maritime history. Exactly one year later Angus Walters took revenge, restoring Nova Scotia pride. Throughout its eighteen-year racing career, *Bluenose* was never defeated.

What concerns us here is the tragedy that occurred during Carnival Week, on the day following the elimination race. Celebrations over, the *Ruby L. Pentz* eased out of her berth at Campbell's Wharf at 11:15 a.m. on Tuesday, October 12, and swung around heading for the mouth of Halifax harbour. Her twenty-three-year-old captain and his crew were already making plans for next year's race, vowing to improve on their seventh-place finish. The popular Cal Lohnes from Rose Bay, also a part owner of the schooner, had already made a name for himself as a successful skipper, having achieved the rank of captain by age eighteen, the youngest in the Lunenburg fleet.

With a strong northerly breeze, the ship made good headway under foresail, jumbo, and jib, towards open water and her home port of Riverport. The mate, Milton Romkey, was at the wheel as they passed through the western passage off McNab's Island approaching the breakwater. The ship's dog, Tog, a large black Labrador, recognizing the alpha sea dog among men, kept close watch beside Captain Lohnes, who stood by on the port side waiting to take the helm. As matters turned out, he was on the wrong side of the ship. A sudden gust of wind caught the loosely hanging

Captain Calvin Joseph Lohnes stands tall on some unknown shore. (Courtesy of the Fisheries Museum of the Atlantic)

mainsail, carrying it to port and dragging the rest of the canvas off the top of the after house with a crack, knocking Cal Lohnes over the rail and into the water. The dreaded alarm "Man overboard!" rang out, for Captain Lohnes could not swim. A first-hand testimony to the tragedy survives in the oral account supplied by friend and crew member Winfred Spindler:

Well, we started for Riverport, and going out of the harbour, quite a little ways out by McNab's Island, we was hoisting the mainsail ... and [Cal] was where he shouldn't have been, over towards the rail – and the canvas swept him overboard. And then when he went overboard we started to tear around, didn't know what to do, so we throwed the [mainboom] crotch, a big piece of hardwood six or eight feet long, to hold the mainboom, we throwed this overboard, but he couldn't get to it ... he couldn't swim. So then they got at a dory. The dory was upside down on the deck, but the mate – I forget who it was – some Romkey, was a little sloppy; he didn't have things in place in case something like that would happen.

So the dory was bottom up, and they got it around, and put it on the rail, put oars into her. We had no tail[1]*, just pushed her over the rail. Before she hit the water I jumped into her just as she left the rail. So I thought to save time. So after I got in, then I went back to the stern, and got things ready. But the tulpins*[2] *weren't there. In a previous interview, I believe I said that one of the tulpins was accidently broken as we were starting off but now I believe one was gone.*

Anyway, ... Joshua Lohnes, the captain's brother, when he came down, he was in the bow and got the oars out. I had to go in the bow to help him because I couldn't row with just one tulpin. So I got in the bow, and that put the dory down, and we couldn't row very fast. The dory was down by the bow. Like they always say, "If." If the tulpin had been there, then I'd have had a pair of oars, and him and I could have got there in time.

---

1 A rope affixed to the transom, used for hoisting dories over the side.

2 Lunenburg County name for tholepin, one of two wooden pins between which an oar plays.

So we started back. We could see him switch around in the water. We kept hollering to him. I could see exactly where he was. I hollered "Keep up! Keep up!" and he kept up quite a while, but when we got there, oh it was very close to him – no more than fifty or seventy-five yards – he went down, his hand up in the air. We came up to where his hand had been in the air, but we couldn't see him. The water was so black in Halifax harbour, looking down we couldn't see him at all. Then we went on board again and started for Riverport. No ... we had to go back first to the wharf to report the loss.

That afternoon in Halifax, the tugs *Togo* and *Weatherspoon* had no success in their grappling work. Nor was a diver able to find any trace of the body.

The *Ruby L. Pentz* arrived at the mouth of the LaHave River late on the day following the loss of her captain. The Canadian Red Ensign fixed halfways to the cross signalled disaster, although the sad news had, of course, preceded their arrival in Riverport. A large crowd waited patiently until the schooner made anchor, and its crew rowed to shore. Four months earlier on June 19, 1920, a disastrous fire had destroyed the entire waterfront, including the wharves. Consequently, the village waterfront presented a blackened backdrop to the bearers of bad news.

Seventeen days passed before RCMP Constable Conrad discovered Cal Lohnes's body floating in Halifax harbour fifty yards northeast of George's Island. The $100 offered by the sailing committee for the recovery of the body was not claimed.

On Sunday, October 31, three funerals were held – a short one at home in Riverport, a second at the Rose Bay Lutheran Church, and a third at the graveside conducted by the deceased's brother Odd Fellows. The Lutheran Church and Sunday school were filled to overflowing, and about five hundred people stood outside. The profusion of tributes and floral displays competed quietly to lessen the grief of the sorrowing family. Rev. F.W. Hirtle conducted the service. Internment followed in the Lower Rose Bay Pioneer Cemetery. Of the occasion, more poignant still, a simple handwritten card from a young lady – "Forget thee, never." – is preserved in an old family album.

A Passing Way of Life

I went to Riverport and there was a vessel laid there by the dock, and the skipper, Byron Levy, wanted me to go with him and I said yes, I'll go ... I was fifteen years old then – deckhand. I came home and my neighbour over here had a horse and wagon, and I got him to take my clothes down to Riverport and we drove out on the wharf and the skipper was there and the men ... something was funny to me ... and I looked around a little ... and I said to the man, "Drive me back home." And he said, "Why, aren't you going?" "No." The skipper come and he turned the horse and he said, "What's the matter?" and I said, "Oh nothing. I'm not going." That vessel went away, but she never came back ... all hands gone ... never heard tell of her ... so I got out under the wire there.

– fisherman Lawson Zinck, Lower Rose Bay,
concerning a waterfront incident in 1916

On June 19, 1920, hastily organized bucket brigades could do little to control the disastrous fire that broke out in Charles Ritcey's waterfront restaurant in Riverport at about 3:30 a.m. A light wind from the east, coupled with a heavy mist, did more than anything else to limit the damage. Even so, the commercial life of the community was brought to a halt. Wharf property, Samuel

Riverport waterfront, viewed from a hastily rebuilt wharf after the fire of June 19, 1920, shows a blackened ruin. The Bank of Montreal (second from left) and the large MacGregor House (to the right of the bank) were spared. After the fire, Ritcey Brothers moved into the MacGregor House. (Photograph by Gilbert Kempton)

Ritcey's general store, Robert Creaser's sail loft, warehouses, the Masonic Quarters, Ritcey Brothers Ltd. store, L.A. Ritcey's Hardware and Furniture, the MacGregor barn, J.F. Risser's store and house, Charles Ritcey's restaurant and ice cream parlour, and Gabriel Zinck's barber shop were all destroyed in the conflagration. But by late summer, rebuilding was already well underway, driven in large measure by the energy and business skill of local entrepreneurs with surnames Ritcey and Creaser. Charles Ritcey and his son Russell were chief among them.

At the time of the great fire, the Grand Banks cod fishery was at its peak, as was the Riverport fishing fleet. A total of twenty-eight schooners sailed out of the village. In his important document *Farewell Old Salts,* Elwood Geldert records twenty-four fishing schooners sailing out of Riverport in 1922. Most of their skippers were local men. By October, according to annual routine, many schooners were already ashore having their bottoms scraped and painted in preparation for next season's frozen bait trip from mid-March to

Part of the Riverport schooner fleet, moored in Ritcey's Cove ca. 1920. The ship on the left has its flag up signifying "Home from the trip." A dory-load of green salted cod makes its way from that vessel toward shore. (Photograph by Gilbert Kempton)

mid-April. Their sails were off, being inspected, and all the dories would have been put in for repairs and repainting.

In addition, a year's work on a salt-banker called for at least two more trips to the Grand Banks, over eight hundred kilometres from Lunenburg. The spring trip lasted through April to about the end of May, dependent upon obtaining a sufficient supply of fresh bait from Newfoundland. There followed the summer or money trip during June and July, when as much as 2,000 to 3,000 quintals (112 pounds to the quintal) of salted fish would be stored in the ship's holds. If, however, the summer trip was not good, a fourth trip might be made in the autumn. Geldert records 5,450 quintals of salt fish, equivalent to about 610,400 pounds, as the record one-trip catch for a single vessel sailing out of Lunenburg in 1926.[1]

About 3,000 fishermen shipped out of Lunenburg that year.

1 According to G.J. Gillespie, in *Bluenose Skipper,* Captain Angus Walters on the *Gilbert B. Walters* holds the all-time Nova Scotia record for a single-trip catch with 790,400 pounds in 1919.

Typically, a vessel's crew consisted of captain, cook, salter, header, throater, sixteen to twenty dorymen (depending on whether eight or ten dories were carried on a full-rigged schooner), and a flunky – a fellow as young as eight to ten, errand boy on the ship and basically a lackey for all of the crew. He received no pay. His main source of income was all the cod tongues he could extract from the fish and salt down in barrels to be sold on his return to port. The dorymen, however, worked as shares-men who would be paid equal shares from the sale of the salted fish once expenses were paid. The captain, usually called the Old Man, was, of course, the big boss whether onshore or at sea, and his word was law. There was only one chair on board a schooner, and that was reserved for the captain. He received a share as well as generous commissions, which made it well worth his while to aim for highliner status. Highliners – captains of ships who brought home the most fish – never had any worries about signing on a crew.

There was no shortage of hard work at sea or on shore. By mid-October of each year, Riverport roadsides and fields were blanketed by crude wooden platforms known as fish flakes. There were "backbreakers" too, where the fish were spread on brush laid over the ground or on frames extending out over the water so that the fish-maker had to stoop to handle the fish and to turn them from time to time. But no matter the arrangement, a constant lookout had to be maintained for a possible downpour, which could spell disaster for the enterprise. Eventually, the cured product was sold to exporters in Halifax for shipment to the West Indies, a portion of which was traded for salt. The salt was obtained from the Turks and Caicos Islands[1] for many years before the Nova Scotia deposits and those on the Îles de la Madeleine were discovered.

According to master shipbuilder Stephen Morash, the cost of a full-sized schooner built in Smith and Rhuland's Lunenburg shipyard in 1908 was $6,400 for hull and spars. In contrast, the

---

1 Recovered from salt pans by evaporation of seawater, this salt is clean and pure.

Dried salted cod lie curing in the sun on hand flakes and backbreakers (right-hand foreground) in Riverport during the early 1920s. (Photograph by Gilbert Kempton)

Bluenose, built in 1920, cost about $35,000, at the time roughly twice as much as any schooner. In *Farewell Old Salts,* Elwood Geldert notes that up to 1930, Smith and Rhuland had built a total of 165 fishing schooners. A great many vessels were also constructed elsewhere in Lunenburg County, especially from 1916 through the early 1920s. In this part of the world you can't tell much from the way a place looks. Captain Frank Smith's compendium *Marine History of the LaHave River* documents the construction of well over one thousand vessels – a few of them full-rigged schooners – in small shipyards at various locations along the LaHave River, such as Bridgewater, LaHave, Dayspring, and Riverport.

Over winter, the schooners were anchored in Ritcey's Cove before becoming thoroughly iced in. The sailing skills of some of the younger sailors were, however, maintained through the depths of that darkest season of the year by yachting over the frozen surface of the LaHave estuary. Then, in mid-March, came the clarion wake-up call as, one after the other, vessels were liberated from the

View from Riverport looking west-northwest shows schooners locked into ice in the LaHave River estuary, ca. 1920. Ice yachting (ice boating) was a popular winter sport in the early 1900s. Note the remains of the burnt-out wharf in the lower right corner. (Photograph by Gilbert Kempton)

ice by the government cutters *Arras* and *Arleux*. Each ship was then escorted, in turn, to the government wharf at Kraut Point where their crews loaded salt in bulk and their complement of dories. A parade of ox-drawn sleighs brought the dories from East LaHave, where they had been overhauled and repainted during winter storage. In a time-honoured ceremony, the sixteen- to seventeen-foot-long dories would be nested upright, generally three or four, and in some cases as many as five each side, depending on the size of the schooner. The life of the entire community revolved around these rites of spring being carried out to the letter.

The Die is Cast: Mate Meets Future Commodore

There is a tide in the affairs of men
Which, taken at the flood, leads on to fortune.
– *Julius Caesar,* Act 4, Scene 2, William Shakespeare

An incident in the fall of 1921 during a trip on the *Annie B. Gerhardt* came close to ending Winfred's life. He would have been better off racing, preferably with Angus Walters on the *Bluenose,* but that was not in the cards. You have only so much good luck in life. It's one of those things that for most mortals seems to be rationed. This time it wasn't a case of a missing tulpin, but something equally trite and essential – a frayed pulley line. Falling from aloft, a topsail sheet block struck him a glancing blow on the right side of the head.

When he came to, apparently two hours later, the first thing he recalled was one of the men taking his pulse. The skipper, Robert (Rattling Boots)[1] Gerhardt, recognized the seriousness of the

1 Captain Gerhardt's nickname stemmed from his practice of always wearing the old-fashioned hobnailed knee-length jack boots that seamen wore before rubber boots were available. For many years, leather jack boots were made (and cured by being filled with linseed oil) at the Reform School in Shelburne.

Winfred sits on the cabin house beside the binnacle on his right, aboard *Annie B. Gerhardt* heading for port following an accident on the Grand Banks in 1921. (Photograph by shipmate Norman Conrad)

accident, and headed for the nearest port – Sydney, Cape Breton. Arriving there a day or so later, shipmates took Winfred to the marine hospital, from which he was transferred to the Victoria General in Halifax. In due course he made a full recovery.

Winfred experienced an epiphany of sorts. He recognized that his everyday life was anchored to a rough-working simplicity linked to the environment. Nothing wrong with that, of course, and he was not about to complain: he chose to follow the sea. However, and despite lacking much formal schooling, he saw that there just might be a way for him to improve his lot in life. Crewmate Norman Conrad provided a means to this end.

Cook on the *Annie B. Gerhardt,* Norman was studying navigation, advanced now to the point where he was ready to take an exam for his Certificate of Competency. In Riverport and District, Norman could hardly be counted as an exception, having received his start from John Mossman[1], a barely literate old shore fisherman from Upper Kingsburg, well known for his uncanny teaching ability. Known as Navigator Johnny, he instructed a good many Riverport and District men who became captains.

During the last trip, Norman practised for his upcoming exam by instructing Winfred in some of the knottier navigational know-how. The learning process might have been more rapid had conditions in school been more favourable. Rattling Boots took a rather dim view of loaning his sextant for sun-shooting practice by crew members, and although the students were keen and apt, free time was a rare commodity for a cook and a doryman aboard a fishing schooner.

Captains at this time had almanacs from which both latitude and longitude could be determined, provided that an accurate sun shot – the elevation of the sun above the horizon at noon – could be obtained. This was accomplished under favourable weather conditions using a sextant. However, to determine longitude, sailors also needed an accurate chronometer set to Greenwich Mean Time (GMT). In one day, sun time changes by one hour for each fifteen degrees of longitude (360 degrees in twenty-four hours). Thus, a ship's position can be fixed by shooting the sun when it is at its zenith above the prime meridian (i.e., Greenwich, U.K.).

"See here," Norman told his severely concussed, bleary-eyed shipmate, as he snapped a prize-winning photograph of the casualty on the cabin house. "When we set you ashore, you'll want something to do while you recover. How about I loan you some notes on navigation, so you can study up some more on the basics? Remember, the key to the whole business is to be able to determine your lat-longs, to be able to fix your position at sea. Guess work, dead reckoning[2], call it what you like, might work pretty good sometimes,

---

1 His name is evidently popular in the area. Another Johnny Mossman from Riverport was in training at the time as a Prohibition Officer.

2 Dead reckoning (also "ded") means deducing one's current position by using a previously determined position.

and when the weather sets in, you don't have much choice."

Of course there was much more to the examination than determination of latitude and longitude. Then, as now, guidebooks on navigation cover everything from position and right of way at sea, to signals and rules concerning shipboard procedure. However, knowing the rules is sometimes not quite good enough when it comes to an examination. A colour-blind colleague of Winfred's in the rum trade, Captain Aubrey Backman, repeatedly failed the examination as administered by a certain agency in Halifax in the 1920s. The examiner apparently focused specifically on a candidate's ability to consistently distinguish between red and green signal lights. Backman eventually passed, but only by courtesy of a different agency, and possibly as a result of different questions entirely.

Winfred was not colour-blind, and he proved a good student, obtaining by the mid-1920s a Certificate of Competency. By then, the most famous era of rum-running in North America was well underway, and, like many fishermen, Winfred, by choice and circumstance, was deeply involved. His career change came about following several mostly forgettable trips on freighters to the Caribbean. During one of those trips on the freighter *Marjorie Hennigar*, Captain Byron Ritcey of Riverport not only helped Winfred further his navigational studies but might have served as a role model. Following the trip Byron gave up freighting for the rum trade and Winfred promptly followed suit. Ritcey was destined to play a key role in rum-running, rising to the informal rank of commodore of what was known as the Banana Fleet, because of the shape of their hulls.

Winfred recalls his wages as mate on *Marjorie Hennigar* in early 1922 as being twenty dollars a month. Also, that the trip was paid by returning a ballast-load of salt taken on at Turks Islands. Two minor incidents on that trip deserve mention, one comic and the other unheard of. The first relates to the antics of Puski, the ship's cat, who it seems caught on fast to the art of fishing.

Puski apparently had the run of the vessel. She almost never got seasick. And in common with others of her species, despite a congenial outward display of disinterest, she was always on the lookout for fish. She developed a great liking for flying fish. She was not alone in this preference, because two of the seven crew members on *Marjorie Hennigar* also hankered after a fresh fry-up of flying fish for breakfast. Puski worked out that the best fishing was to be had at night, when there was no competition between her and raucous creatures with large wings. The two sailors were in the habit of collecting the piscine manna during their early morning watch. Unknown to them, Puski was also standing watch. A sudden drop in numbers of flying fish on deck puzzled them, until one morning they discovered a large telltale heap of regurgitated fish. Puski, the watch cat, would pay in full for her gluttonous appetite, and for the rest of the trip she was confined below decks at night.

Then there was the rather more serious incident concerning fire on board the ship. According to Winfred:

The strangest thing happened during that same trip. I was mate at the time. We had six, no, seven in the crew, I think, and we were headed for San Juan, Puerto Rico. So we were six or seven hundred miles from Puerto Rico, somewhere in the Gulf Stream, sailing along on a fine day, you know, really hot, one of the real hot days. And there wasn't much wind, and the mainsail was hitting back and forth. Anyway, the man at the wheel, steering, he sung out, "Fire aloft! Fire in the main mast!"

I couldn't believe it. I looked up, and the fire and smoke was coming out way up at the top of the masthead. So, as the mate, the only thing I knew was I couldn't take a bucket of water up the rigging, so I grabbed an old coat and soaked it in water, and then I went up the rigging pretty good and put the coat over the fire. It wasn't a big fire, but big enough. Anyway, I got it out aloft and then somebody hollered out, "Fire on deck!"

And here, the stay sail – one of the small sails that was spread out on the deck – some sparks struck that, setting it on fire. We saw it right away, so it didn't burn much. But it's pretty hard for some people to believe that, and how it happened.

But the way we figured it out, it had to be iron against iron, to cause friction and the sparks on rope. The rocking motion of the vessel and the friction made a fire on the rope lashing on the mast. But I'd never heard of that before.

Prohibition

Tis easy and free for us boys out at sea
Way-o, whiskey and gin!
Pigs will all fly when the country goes dry
Give us the word, we'll run the rum in.

– From "The Smuggler's Chanty"
Joseph Chase Allen

After capturing Jamaica in 1655, the British Admiralty was swift to introduce a diluted ration of rum to replace their traditional and perishable beer. The British found rum to be a compelling diversion on the lower decks. At the very least, it provided a welcome alternative to putrid water during long voyages.

In *A History of the World in Six Glasses,* Tom Standage elegantly reviews the evolution of rum as the first global drink. It originated as rumbullion, a natural brew formed by airborne yeast spores reacting with discarded molasses and cane juice from mid-seventeenth-century sugar mills in the Caribbean. It all began when Christopher Columbus introduced sugar cane to Hispaniola (the island now shared by Haiti and Dominican Republic) during his second voyage to the Americas late in 1493. When distilled, the drink's potency increased its popularity such that, over time, a substantial trade developed between the Atlantic Provinces and the West Indies. Ironically, the Americans played the most important role in delivering rum to the Atlantic Provinces by dodging British trade barriers. In the Maritimes, rum flowed freely. So much so that through five hundred years it has been a significant force in politics, religion, and socio-economics. In *A Burning Mercy: Rum in the Atlantic Provinces,* James Moreira serves up fascinating details about the practice. Of all types on offer, Jamaican rum, being doubly distilled, commanded the most respect and the highest prices.

Fast forward to 2014, when, at the World Rum Awards held in London, Ironworks Bluenose Black Rum, distilled at the Ironworks Distillery in the old blacksmith shop in Lunenburg, earned a Gold Medal as the world's best dark rum. At this competition, judging centres around the taste of the rum and the design of the bottle and packaging. Tasting (nose, palate, and finish) is conducted blind in three rounds by a group of specialist drinks retailers, bartenders/mixologists, hoteliers, distillers, and leading journalists. As for design, leading international design experts assess entries on the quality of the design, innovative use of materials, and production techniques.

The blacksmith shop was originally Thomas Walters' Marine Blacksmith. When construction of the distillery began in 2009, many empty whisky bottles were discovered beneath the floor. Several years earlier, Gregg Ernst, the last blacksmith to work the smithy from 1996 to 2004, also uncovered relics of the rum-running era, including an empty rum keg.

That the blacksmith shop was probably a favourite haunt of rum-runners makes sense, considering the amount of iron required to keep the ships running. The old Lunenburg Temperance Hall, a stone's throw distant on Hobson Street, is of course long gone. But the irony of it all is unmistakable.

Inevitably, during the eighteenth century, as excesses of drinking occurred, a backlash developed along frontiers of the New World, and calls for temperance were insistently loud and clear.

However, it would be an uphill battle because at an early date a substantial proportion of the population of the United States had subscribed to the words of Benjamin Franklin, as noted by Joseph Furnas in *The Life and Times of The Late Demon Rum,* in the song made popular ca. 1745.

'Twas honest old Noah first planted the vine,
And mended his morals by drinking its wine;
And justly the drinking of water decry'd,
For he knew that all Mankind, by drinking it dy'd.

In 1847, the U.S. Supreme Court gave states full power to either prohibit or regulate the sale of liquor. In eastern Canada, following the Great War of 1914-1918, fish prices dropped disastrously and the door suddenly opened to fishermen willing, for mainly economic reasons, to make the remarkable switch to smuggling. It happened on January 16, 1919, when, after more than a century of vigorous agitation by mainly Protestant groups to promote temperance, the liquor-banning Eighteenth Amendment to the American Constitution was passed in the U.S. legislature. This made the production, transportation, and sale of alcohol illegal in the United States. This was followed exactly one year later by the National Prohibition Act, commonly called the Volstead Act after its sponsor Andrew Volstead, which set out how to enforce the Eighteenth Amendment. The Volstead Act came into force on January 16, 1920, and held until its repeal on April 7, 1933.

The impossibility of enforcing Prohibition was pretty much evident right from the outset. Ships, planes, and wheeled vehicles of every description were hastily mobilized to cash in. Enormous commitments of time, effort, and money were invested to capture and prosecute offenders. However, for successful bootleggers, scofflaws, and rum-runners, there was big money to be made as this huge new industry opened up, especially for insiders at the higher levels. The United States Coast Guard (USCG) was assigned the monumental charge of policing the entire American coastline of the Pacific, Atlantic, Gulf of Mexico, and the Great Lakes against the flow of illegal liquor. Not to be denied a piece of the action, a veritable host of tiny Nova Scotia communities also became involved. Prohibition would be a costly fourteen-year social experiment for the American government, although the economic benefit for many Canadians, ordinary and otherwise, would prove substantial.

Some venturesome Europeans got in on the act early on, legally shipping liquor to islands in the Bahamas (for example, Nassau), St. Pierre off Newfoundland, and even directly to locations off the U.S. coast near major population centres. A vastly greater volume crossed the Canada-U.S. border. After all, in Canada during most of the Prohibition era, liquor exports were not prohibited by Ottawa. It was not until 1930 that parliament banned liquor exports "to countries under Prohibition." This made-in-heaven hypocrisy translated to an estimated hundred million dollars' worth of liquor crossing the border annually during the early 1930s, according to figures given in Lloyd McKenna's *Atlantic Canadian Rum Runners*.

One highly successful land-based operation was organized by Harry and Sam Bronfman in Yorkton, Saskatchewan. Early in Prohibition, the brothers established the Canada Pure Drug Company, which imported "ardent spirits" (ethyl alcohol) to manufacture supposed medicines. From Yorkton, it was but a short step to export the product, generally in diluted form, to markets in Canada and the United States. American businessman Joseph Patrick (Joe) Kennedy Sr. – the founder of the Kennedy political dynasty and the father of President John F. Kennedy – was a major rival of the Bronfmans in efforts to obtain distribution rights throughout North America. Despite huge investment in the legal importation of liquor, Kennedy and the Bronfmans were reportedly deeply involved in the illegal importation and distribution of alcohol.

The Volstead Act stipulated that alcohol could only be purchased for religious, military, industrial, and medical purposes. In retrospect, the intent of the ruling challenges belief. A physician's authorization was required even for purchasing a bottle of beer. Of course, there were ways around the problem, for sympathetic souls were seldom hard to find.

Ed Morrison, a radio operator on a rum-runner boat, in Lunenburg between trips in the early 1930s, explains in McKenna's *Atlantic Canadian Rum Runners* how the system worked. He and two fellow crew members, deciding that cold beer was preferable to a hot rum toddy, visited a doctor with the plea that they were not feeling well and were in need of a little tonic. A prescription for a dozen bottles was duly provided. Because it was raining, the kindly doctor phoned the police chief, who provided a cell as well as playing cards for the trio so that "no one would see [them] walking around with it that way." Conveniently, the liquor outlet was in the same building as the jail.

Much of the liquor from Canada flowed into the U.S. from the Great Lakes region, particularly through Detroit. Charles and Marty Gervais give a vivid picture of the practice in this region in *The Rumrunners*. The balance was delivered by rum-running boats from the Maritimes, of which there were about seventy-five operating along the Atlantic seaboard in 1930. Most of these ships were manned, captain and crew, from Lunenburg and Riverport. More than a dozen, including those of the Banana Fleet, sailed out of Riverport (and Liverpool and Yarmouth) bound for Rum Row – offshore between Boston and Atlantic City.

Canadian Maritime rum-runners loaded up mainly in the Caribbean and St. Pierre and Miquelon, although they occasionally found it convenient to take on Scotch whisky in the British crown colonies of the Bahamas (Nassau), British Honduras (Belize), and Bermuda. The entire business operated under the direction of wealthy, well-connected groups of American financiers. Known as syndicates, in many instances they worked with organized crime groups. The most notorious financier of them all was, of course, Al Capone in Chicago.

Maritime rum-runners were not overly concerned about the

identity of their paymasters. Neither crew nor rum-runner captains knew – apart from some middlemen – who was paying them. On average, it was a month-long trip from Riverport or Lunenburg to St. Pierre to load up, steam to the American coast, make a drop, and return to Nova Scotia. A completely trouble-free trip could be made in as little as nine days. The men were glad to get the work. They viewed their occupation much the same as they would any other form of employment. While they liked the adventure, they also liked the payoffs. In the 1920s, the lowliest crew member earned $75 during the average month-long trip, plus a $150 bonus at the end of each successful run. This, in contrast to the $75 he might receive for a full season's fishing. A rum-runner captain and first mate might pull down ten times the wage of a crew member.

In *The Atlantic Privateers,* John Leefe might equally well have been referring to Maritime rum-running communities when he concludes, "So, here it is, the phenomenon of privateering in a nutshell. It was not comparable to piracy although a few overzealous privateersmen came awfully close to crossing the line separating them. Similarly, it was not conducted by ruthless adventurers nor by dashing naval heroes, but rather by seamen and ships' masters who would far sooner have been following more peaceful pursuits. None made a fortune from privateering although a few businessmen were able to sustain some considerable financial gain. Finally, the law of the sea rather than being abused was given more careful prominence through privateering for, in the best tradition of British justice, the onus lay on the captor to prove the 'guilt' of the vessel and cargo brought to court. In fact, it was [a] respectable occupation carried on by respectable men, men who had long before learned to adapt themselves to conditions which the sea and their governments imposed upon them."

The life of our Maritime rum-runners, though rather less romantic and publically applauded, in many ways resembled that of privateers who operated out of Liverpool, Nova Scotia, during the early nineteenth century. King of that swashbuckling fraternity, Enos

Collins owned the fabulously successful *Liverpool Packet*, which held a letter of marque (a government license to engage in privateering) out of that port. In later years Collins founded, on his winnings, the Halifax Banking Company (now the CIBC) and by 1871 was considered the richest man in Canada. His captain, Samuel Barss, shared in the profits according to the pecking order established in the Vice-Admiralty Prize Court in Halifax. Presiding Prize Court Judge was Sir Alexander Croke, by all accounts a stuffy high Tory British aristocrat who contributed in his own inimitable way, as did Collins and Barss, to Maritime heritage. To wit: Gorsebroook, now the site of Saint Mary's University, was the estate of Enos Collins; upon retirement, Barss purchased a farm to grow apples on the grounds of what is now the Agricultural Research Station in Kentville; and with his substantial winnings, Croke amassed the estate presently occupied by Dalhousie University and King's College.

Whereas privateering and rum-running were conducted as business enterprises, privateering was deemed a legal practice as it was carried out in wartime. Although it must be admitted that warlike conditions likewise held during Maritime rum-running, the legality of that enterprise ended with the export of the commodity offshore. Thus, in contrast to privateering, the considerable wealth won by rum-runners was (except perhaps for the brewers and distillers themselves) in large measure hidden throughout the country in enterprises which do not care particularly to advertise their origins. Who knows how many fish plants, bus lines, breweries, banks, drug companies, and real estate agencies might have been seeded from a rum-runner's purse. Someone ought to conduct a survey.

Temperance societies were very well organized in Canada, and in Atlantic Canada they worked tirelessly to try and bring about total Prohibition. In fact, Prohibition in Canada predates the American version. Details of how exactly this situation came about are given by Daniel Francis in *Closing Time*. In brief, it began courtesy of the Canadian Temperance Act (also known as the Scott Act) of 1878, which provided an option for municipalities, by plebiscite, to subscribe to Prohibition. Twenty years later, an official (though not binding) federal referendum resulted in a narrow vote in favour of prohibition, Quebec being the only province to opt out.

In Atlantic Canada, enthusiasm for provincial Prohibition peaked during World War I but decreased in the mid-1920s. The experiment was discarded by Newfoundland in 1924, New Brunswick in 1927, and Nova Scotia in 1929, whereas Prince Edward Island was dogged by a bone-dry statute until 1938.

As in the U.S., the quandary was how to enforce the legislation. Despite the intended effect, Prohibition actually increased the demand for alcohol. Even after the end of Prohibition in the U.S. in late 1933, smuggling booze into America continued to be an attractive proposition due to the demand for high-priced liquors. From then on, however, the focus of attention swung toward supplying rum to the many thirsty customers along the Canadian east coast. Here, despite the establishment of the Nova Scotia Liquor Control Board in April 1930, as the official agency for the purchase, transport, and sale of liquor, the rum trade remained viable until World War II heralded the end of the era.

It might reasonably be argued that little has changed since then, and that a residue of lawlessness left over from the rum-running era plagues law enforcement efforts today. The new prohibition is narcotics, but the old game of cat and mouse plays on, deadly for some unfortunate participants. Headlines report almost daily on gang warfare, smuggling, distribution of contraband tobacco, political maneuvering, corruption, and disrespect of the law – all of which echo commonplace events during the rum-running era. In *The Long Thirst*, Thomas Coffey notes that some dope dealers are descendants of liquor dealers during Prohibition, and he suggests that by opting for strict law enforcement "the agencies responsible for stopping the drug traffic are actually being used to perpetuate it."

Book 2
Rum-Running

Maritime Madness

Rum-runner ships awash with brine,
The wind a-blowing free
As we sailed along with loaded holds
Across the miles of sea.
The cutter's beam across our bow,
A bullet in the stack.
Reverse the engines – a screen of smoke
No chance of turning back.
Elude the sharks pursuing us
Sail in to the open beach
Jettison our load – then out to sea –
Far from the cutter's reach.
This was the life, now I look back
And wish for the long ago
Oh to be back, on a rum-runner's deck
With my friends along Rum Row.

– "Nostalgia," Don Miller

Strictly defined, rum-running, or bootlegging, is the time-tested practice of escaping restrictions applied to the manufacture, distribution, and sale of alcohol in North America. Most communities

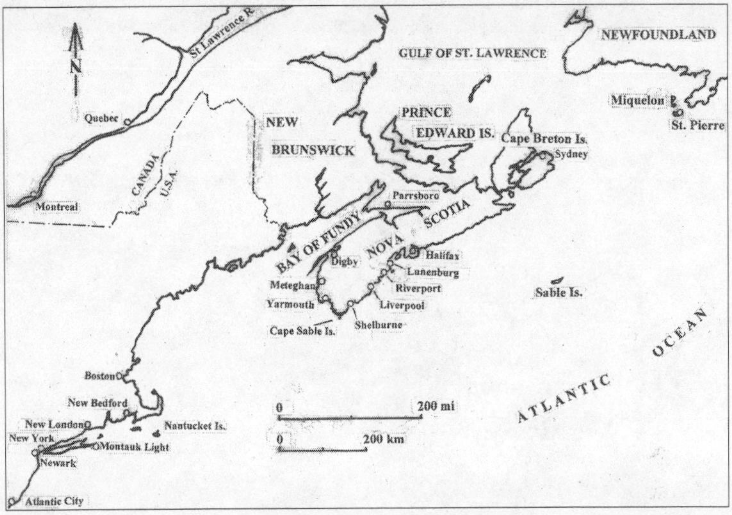

This map shows several of the many Nova Scotia communities involved in the rum trade.

in the Maritimes, especially those along the coast, wasted no time in becoming involved. After all, thousands of miles of complicated coastline made it ideal for hiding out from, or otherwise eluding, authorities in search of offenders.

The rum trade spelled big business for Americans and Canadians alike, even as both countries experimented by banning the consumption of alcohol. In the Maritime Provinces, the scale of efforts to circumvent Prohibition laws in the U.S. amounted to a major domestic industry. For folks on the French Islands of St. Pierre and Miquelon off Newfoundland, where liquor importation was legal, Prohibition proved an economic godsend in the face of the Depression and the decline of the salt-bank fishery.

All types of schooners sailed to the Caribbean to take on rum. The largest (tanker-type) could handle up to 60,000 gallons. Returning to the Atlantic seaboard, smaller vessels would rendezvous with such a mother ship and ferry the contraband ashore for later distribution. Customers were not hard to find. But although

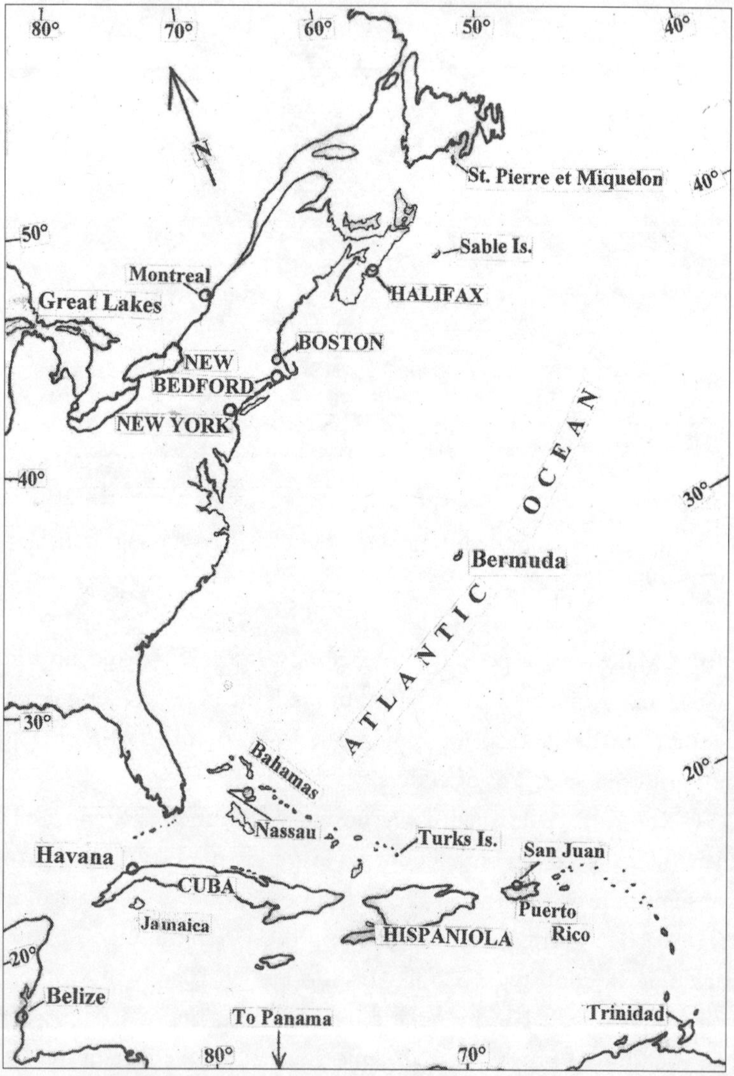

This map shows the range of rum-running activities carried out by ships of the Banana Fleet and other syndicates.

rum was a generic term for all spirts, it was not the drink that most Americans preferred. To satisfy the American market, Maritime schooners loaded up with exotic liquors and champagne brought to St. Pierre from Europe, as well as high-profit gin, rye, and bourbon whiskies, huge amounts of which were legally exported to this prohibition-free island by Canadian distilleries such as those run by the Bronfmans.

Liquor was inexpensive on St. Pierre, so fishing schooners made sure not to seek shelter there during severe weather. Instead, the practice was to anchor in the lee of the island to avoid a royal drunk. Different rules applied to rum-running schooners from Nova Scotia. In the early years they would usually load up from warehouses, including those stocked by Canadian distillers, on St. Pierre. Cargo holds were packed with burlap bags and/or wooden boxes containing twelve bottles each. In St. Pierre, that cargo was declared as destined for a Nova Scotia port, but in reality it would be shipped directly to Rum Row along the American coast. The term originated during Prohibition and refers to a line of ships loaded with liquor either anchored or hovering just beyond the offshore territorial limit. On the Atlantic seaboard, by far the busiest market was located off the New Jersey coast. The United States Coast Guard (USCG) called these rum-runner ships blacks because of their common, hazardous practice of running without lights.

Once at sea, the ship's name might be changed, but there was no going ashore until this mobile liquor store reached its destination and discharged its cargo, generally into contact boats capable of speeds in excess of twenty-five knots, though in some cases directly ashore. Rarely was a sale made on the high seas to potential customers in the Atlantic steamship lanes. For contact boats, the rendezvous would be at a pre-arranged location outside the territorial limit. That limit was three nautical miles, until a 1924 treaty between the U.S. and Great Britain extended it to twelve nautical miles, or one hour's sailing time from the coastline. The USCG read this to mean that any rum-runner was subject to seizure if in contact with an American craft which was within one hour's steaming distance from shore. This proved to be a rather troublesome concept, given the continual arms race for faster boats between the rum-runners and Canadian and American Preventive Services. Although the Canadian Customs Preventive Services originated in the late nineteenth century, it was only in the early 1930s that it began to deploy numerous ships and men against smugglers. However, throughout Prohibition, their American counterpart in the USCG played a vastly greater role in efforts to constrain the activities of rum-runners.

In the early 1920s, schooners were the usual rum-runners on Rum Row, and they did most of the over-the-side selling to speedy, small motorized contact boats. By the late 1920s, schooners were replaced by motorized craft equipped with wireless in addition to the usual sextant, charts, compass, and chronometer. In many instances, such heavily laden craft risked making drops directly on shore. According to Lloyd McKenna in *Atlantic Canadian Rum Runners,* rum-runners used wireless cryptograms in ship-to-shore communications to help solve contact and delivery problems. These proved difficult for the USCG to break, especially during the 1920s. However, as time went on, increasingly vigilant patrol and enforcement procedures of the Marine Police, Customs, and the USCG became a growing threat up and down the Atlantic Seaboard.

Traffic to the American market from the Maritimes was totally governed by syndicates based principally in New Jersey and New York. Fronts for these organizations reliably paid Maritime rum-runners at their home ports following a successful landing of their illicit cargos. Besides St. Pierre and Miquelon, various other foreign countries – including Bermuda, Bahamas, Cuba, and British Honduras (Belize) – served as convenient trans-shipment centres for rum from Canada. Syndicate agents acted swiftly and efficiently to supply lawyers and bail wherever and whenever needed, and to generally assist the crews of rum-runners. The fronts were richly financed, a situation which doubtless contributed to the laid-back attitude among many of the characters directing operations. Their generous license in this respect allowed them to play the fool on occasion. To illustrate, fast forward to the late 1930s to find Winfred on board *Atacama,* steaming a mere three thousand miles or so to South America to pick up a shipment of liquor intended for resale at U.S. destinations.

On one trip, we stopped off in Hamilton, Bermuda, for supplies and fuel on the way to [Belize] to pick up a load. Going along we ran into the tail end of a hurricane before we got there. And I kept going too long. We were in a race with Joey Himmelman. I'm not quite sure why, but we were. And it started to get pretty wild, going hard, and the boat was light, had no ballast, so I said to the mate – I think it was Calvin Silver – I said, "We got to keep going because if we don't, Joey Himmelman will be there ahead of us."

So we kept steaming, and after a while she was pitching so hard on the water that the men were being thrown out of their bunks. And they couldn't sleep or rest on the floor so some of them, they came back in the cabin. That was all right. So next morning it got so tough we had to stop for a while. Then the cook came back and said, "Skipper, the water's all gone. We got no water."

"Well," I said, "now that's something funny."

"No," he said, "there's no water in the tanks. Everything is dry."

Well, as luck would have it, we had half a barrel and we had it tied to the rail in case of necessity. And I said to the mate, go and see if you can find any water back there. Well, he found the half barrel of water. We were only about two days from Bermuda. So when we got in, they checked up. We had two 500-gallon tanks, one in the hold where we kept the liquor, and the other one in the forecastle. Seems like we pitched so bad and the water slopped back and forth so hard that it broke the tanks. Hard to believe it.

But I'm getting ahead in my yarn. Anyway, we got in in the morning, around daylight. The other boat came in around dinnertime. But he had stopped and did not steam along like we did. So we let the owners know what happened. We needed some repairs, new tanks. Well, they said that they'd fix us up temporarily, and they'd send away to Lunenburg because Bermuda was a pretty expensive place to get anything done.

It was all a bit of a joke. You see, the owners told me to make sure not to let anyone get there ahead of me. They said that as a joke. They paid for that – quite a few dollars. Calvin Silver was mate, because the fishing was poor at that time. He was mate with us quite a while at the time. And he says to me the next day, "I didn't say anything." But I knew what he meant. We should have stopped before. He had way more experience than I had. He was a captain of a Grand Banks fishing vessel and had lots of experience.

But I enjoyed Bermuda. I really liked that place – better than St. Pierre.

The sea leg from the Maritimes to Bermuda is a relatively straight run south, requiring few sun shots. But even for an experienced navigator, peering through the binnacle while driving on through the black of night in heavy seas may have shaken a few nerves, not to mention stomachs. Small wonder then, that raising Bermuda left a memorably happy mark.

Unfortunately, Winfred left scant details concerning the results of his mission to Belize. The westerly sea path to that particular enclave, crouched on the eastern shore of Central America, presents more obstacles to navigation than the run to Bermuda. Evidently the trip to Belize was successful, for *Atacama* managed to dodge the numerous islands and reefs along the way as well as the USCG patrols. Perhaps later, like the captain of the famous Lunenburg rum-runner *I'm Alone,*[1] Winfred may have delivered some of his cargo to New Orleans, the wettest place in the U.S.A. We will never know for sure. But there's no question he knew his way around the

---

1 *I'm Alone* was shot to bits and sunk by the USCG cutter *Dexter* in March 1929 in the Gulf of Mexico, far from U.S. territorial waters. The resulting Canadian lawsuit outlasted Prohibition and ended in a formal apology by the U.S. government, a token payment of $25,000 to Canada and $25,666.50 compensation to the crew of *I'm Alone*. Captain John Thomas Randell got $7,906; the boatswain's widow $10,000; the balance went to the eighteen crewmen and Randell.

Caribbean and Central American ports as well as the innumerable coastal nooks and crannies along the Atlantic Seaboard that make Nova Scotia so ideal for the smuggler's purpose.

Winfred would do well financially in his younger years, more so certainly in rum-running than fishing. And despite free spending habits, he managed somehow to invest a good deal of his winnings in Ma Bell (American Telephone and Telegraph Company) and similar shiny blue chip stock offerings. His sister Helen was apparently complicit in some of those money-making schemes, for my brother George recalls the two of them on more than one occasion discussing the status of Ma Bell – a long-time favourite stock – while seated in the family pew moments before the morning church service began in Trinity United.

Many books have been written on rum-running along the Atlantic Seaboard, among them an excellent overview by James Morrison and James Moreira in *Tempered by Rum: Rum in the History of the Maritime Provinces*. Hugh Corkum's *On Both Sides of the Law* tells stories of those times "straight from the shoulder and source," and ranks as one of the best first-hand accounts. With respect to Winfred Spindler's role, as a sometime shipmate with Corkum, his experiences were doubtless common to many of those already on record. However, like most old warriors, he was reluctant to name names, or to supply much by way of dates and details for fear that information might reach the ears of a squealer. Nevertheless, time and distance have conspired to release a few stories about the times and trials of Winfred and those of his family.

Thou Shalt Not

Dirty money, it's the worst kind
Dirty money, it's a bad sign
Something isn't right on the sea of life.

– Chorus to "Dirty Money,"
written by Hank Middleton for
Lunenburg Dinner Players production
The Run for Rum

In his article "Rum in the Maritimes' Economy during the Prohibition Era," Ernest Forbes describes the effects of the rum trade in various Maritime communities as mixed. However, he concludes, "The rum trade was not the basic cause of the fishermen's difficulties." Despite the hazards, rum-runners liked the money and the adventure, and no matter the moral sanctions encountered at home, they made light of any possible religious transgression. The most hilarious everyday hypocrisy in all this concerned the routine clearing of Customs. Each time passing through Customs, a captain was obliged to name the port to which he was coming from or to which his ship was bound. When asked if he always told the truth, Captain Winfred Spindler replied, in his typically understated manner, "Well, I kissed the Bible so often, my lips got sore. But you told

Trinity United Church with the spire on the left, Upper Rose Bay, ca. 1924. Then the Methodist Church, it often hosted temperance society meetings, like the one described below. The large house (right of centre) belonged to Dr. Geoffrey Barss, M.D. (Photograph by Gilbert Kempton)

Customs whatever you could, near as you could, to the truth. If it got too tough, sometimes you had to tell lies … but not too much." Interrogation by St. Peter at the Pearly Gates might follow a similar script.

While rum-running bolstered family and small-town community fortunes during the Depression, religious and community leaders recognized only the real failings of the practice. Witness the November 30, 1924, occasion of a mass meeting of the citizens of Riverport, Rose Bay, and adjoining sections held in the Methodist Church[1] in Upper Rose Bay, Sunday evening (as reported in the *Progress Enterprise*, December 3, 1924). To appreciate the scale of the event, one must realize that this meeting was just one of several being held throughout Riverport and District.

1 Which in 1925 would become Trinity United Church.

Eight-year-old Charles Ritcey's Certificate of Membership shows he was one of 132 Cheerful Workers in the Band of Hope, Riverport, Nova Scotia, in 1892. Originating in England in 1847, the Band of Hope was dedicated to teaching working-class children the value of abstaining from alcohol. (Courtesy of Charlotte Boates)

Reverend Percy M. Hartley, representative of the three churches – Methodist, Presbyterian, and Lutheran – in the Protestant community of Riverport presides over the meeting at the close of the regular church service. Reverend Dr. H.R. Grant, the redoubtable Head of the Moral Reform Forces in Nova Scotia and General Secretary of the Social Service Council of the province, is chief speaker. In addition to his regular duties as a clergyman, Rev. Grant is the undisputed leader of the drys in Nova Scotia; he is renowned for his unremitting efforts throughout Prohibition to recruit spies in various Maritime communities in order to catch bootleggers. With a deep sense of satisfaction, Rev. Hartley notes that the pews, a good many of which are occupied by local Cheerful Workers of the Band of Hope, are filled to capacity. (Members of the Band of Hope were dedicated to educating children and young people about sobriety and total abstinence from alcohol.) Close on the heels of these two spokesmen of God are Rev. Carl Sorenson of the Lutheran Church and Rev. S.P. Archibald of the Presbyterian Church, who will serve as secretary for the meeting.

Not entirely certain of the composition and mood of this mixed congregation, Rev. Hartley softens them up with an introductory prayer. Then, championing the expression of moral outrage intended by this meeting, he proceeds to invoke the wisdom of the Old Testament prophets who, it seems, without exception strongly endorsed prohibition of alcholic liquors. Even old Adam comes in for honorable mention for the virtues of his preferred ale. Predictably, this draws a low rumble of approval from the otherwise sober assembly. The stage is set for the main speaker.

Rev. Grant launches into an impassioned address to the citizens, focusing at first on temperance reform and the need for education. Then, at considerable length, he outlines the laws both provincial and federal, relating to Prohibition. Reverends Sorenson and Archibald take turns, railing on about the devilish pleasantries of bootleggers and the sinfulness of dirty money, urging listeners to do everything in their power to stamp out the accursed traffic.

Much the same message, of course, was at the time being fed to younger captive Protestant audiences in Sunday schools. The Temperance Movement was close to its peak when the Great War broke out. Dozens if not hundreds of church groups and societies in the Maritimes, as elsewhere throughout Canada, were committed to Prohibition.

According to Furnas in *The Life and Times of The Late Demon Rum,* the poems of Dr. Charles Jewett are typical of the literature distributed by Temperance agencies. An example:

They put molasses many an hour
Into vats and let it sour;
When it is as sour as swill,

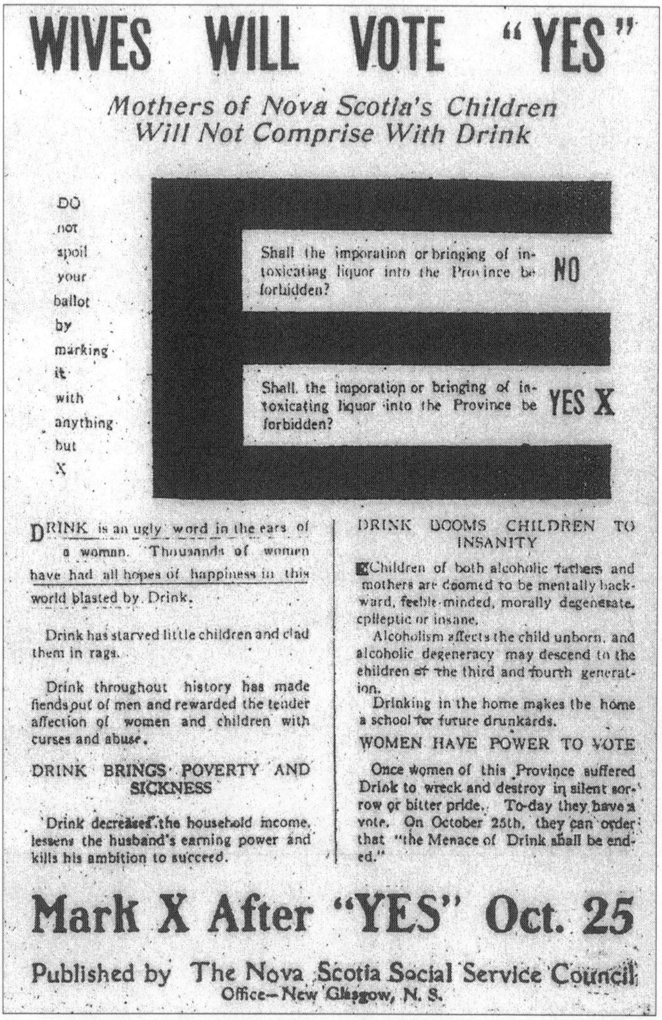

In March 1918, an amendment to the War Measures Act introduced Prohibition throughout Canada. But problems with enforcement and increases in smuggling led to amending the Canada Temperance Act to allow provincial plebiscites on the question of Prohibition. This plebiscite form concerning Prohibition was distributed by the Nova Scotia Social Services Council in 1920. On October 25, 1920, Nova Scotians voted for Prohibition 82,573 to 23,953, the highest support ever recorded in the province. (Courtesy of the Fisheries Museum of the Atlantic)

Then they pour it in a still.
Under it they put the fire
Till it burns up high and higher
Now the poison hot and strong
Trickles through the pipe along,
Till it drops into the cask.
Little reader, do you ask
Why they turn molasses sweet
That is given us to eat
Into rum? I'll tell you why:
'Tis that foolish men may buy
And drink the poison stuff and die.

By 9:30 p.m., it was established beyond reasonable doubt that rum-running and smuggling were on the increase in Riverport and District, and that the Provincial Temperance and the Inland Revenue Acts were being openly violated by lawless fellow citizens. This remarkable meeting went as far as possible to fulfill its mandate (as recorded in the *Progress Enterprise*) that "the Citizens of Riverport Memorialize [demand] the Provincial and Federal Governments to Enforce Laws Against Rum-Running and Smuggling of Liquors." Thus, in the presence of five hundred or more citizens, a series of recommendations were swiftly adopted, among them: that the will of Nova Scotia prohibitionists be respected, and that the Nova Scotia Temperance Act and the Inland Revenue Act be vigorously enforced by provincial and federal authorities. Specific criticism was levelled at "our Federal Member" (William Duff, MP, and Mayor of Lunenburg) for his financial interest in rum-running and for his support of the right of British-owned ships and shipowners to transport liquor to points outside territorial waters.

This gathering of the converted proved, in retrospect, little more than a kangaroo court convened to decry inroads being made by demon rum and its supporters upon a respectable God-fearing community. This fact was established well before the meeting ended. True, several sea captains served the church as trustees and stewards, but of the lot, only Skipper Dan was there, as his young wife, Mary Dan, was quick to point out. As she might well have added of her husband, Master Mariner Captain Daniel Romkey – surely an anomaly in the community – "He has his principles, and he continues to fish for fish." In short, there were no rum-runners in attendance. A foregone conclusion, as several elderly matrons sniffed. For the odds were that their own men either were boycotting the meeting or were away who knows where, bottle fishing.

There were some church ladies among the gathering that evening who may have considered rum more effective than chicken soup for warding off a cold. But, if they did, they kept their voices down. After all, this was an open public forum, and reputations were on the line. The risk of becoming a social outcast was real. Most women may not have approved of smuggling, of course, but they would be unlikely to be counted among the squealers. Their home in Riverport and District was their little piece of Heaven, though it might have seemed at times that even Heaven was not without its liabilities. Although women were effectively excluded from political forums at the time, the church was one venue where they had opportunities to express themselves and their concerns, despite circumstances beyond their control. But in the end, there were mouths to feed and somehow the bills had to be paid.

The pretenses held by righteous citizens of Riverport and District, as elsewhere throughout the Maritime Provinces and the rest of Canada, would endure throughout many long thirsty years, ostensibly until 1929 in Nova Scotia's case, when the experiment ended. However, with the machinery already in place, rum-running continued on a large scale in Atlantic Canada right up to the outbreak of World War II. Throughout this entire era, many folks were reluctant to talk about the popular occupation of smuggling, except perhaps to deplore the rum-runners and their dirty money. And I can attest that, to this very day, some wrinkled old lips remain sealed.

Willoughby Ritcey

In retrospect, public antipathy toward informers can be readily understood. Decades after the fact, however, the reluctance of some knowledgeable folks to unlock their memories on this and related issues and incidents during rum-running is downright curious. Yet such is the case to this day.

For example, by the time I graduated from Lunenburg County Academy in 1955, my ignorance was ever so slightly diluted with knowledge, if not wisdom. That year, plans were made to include in the school's yearbook biographical sketches of several Lunenburg County notables. Our history teacher, the popular Robert Campbell, suggested that I and a schoolmate, Lena Croft, contribute a short article on Willoughby Ritcey, the entrepreneur and businessman from Riverport. Willoughby was all of that and more, Lena and I agreed, and so we set to work outlining his accomplishments and community contributions.

It turns out that even to mention a rum-runner would have been a major breach of protocol for the Sea Gull yearbook. Consequently, the final edition of our article omitted all mention of the empire-building efforts of this remarkable man. At a stroke, any trace of rum-running was washed from his past. The sealed lips policy of some rum-runner captains seems to have been contagiously enduring. This much was evident early in my research in Riverport and District in the lead-up to this book. Consider, too, the town website (riverport.org) provides a partial list of vessels calling Riverport their home port over the years. That number, as given, totals fifty-five. But the last time I looked it did not include a single rum-runner. Most rum-runners, like their privateer counterparts a full century earlier, scarcely qualify as Robin Hoods, but they might evoke empathy among an audience drawn to stories of adventure, particularly when they involve familiar characters like themselves. After all, no one is perfect, are they? Liverpool, Nova Scotia, now honours its former privateers during Privateer Days, signalling public recognition of their important role in Maritime history.

On the whole, there were relatively few problems in Riverport with government inspectors and preventive officers in the Department of National Revenue, and despite the potential for squealers in any crowd, very few seizures were made. Many small drops made it safely through to meet local demand, including supplying the fuel for regular parties held at W.R.'s cottage at Oxner's Beach in Lower LaHave and elsewhere at meetings in Riverport and District. Winfred was one of the regular suppliers. In his words, "I'd sneak some in pretty well every trip. Everybody was trying to make some money. But you had to always keep a sharp lookout for Johnny Mossman, the prohibition-revenue officer in Riverport. You'd never know where and when he would show up. He took his job seriously."

Small wonder then that rum-running became a way of life in the area, if for no other reason than to smooth the raspy throats of our well-moneyed God-fearing neighbours to the south in the U.S., while at the same time providing for modest domestic needs.

In view of the money to be made, the risk of getting caught was considered well worth it. One successful drop more than paid for a mishap or two.

On the other hand, the various provincial and municipal preventive agencies brought in revenue by levelling fines, seizing cargoes of liquor, and auctioning off impounded rum boats – which more often than not were purchased at fire sale prices by their original owners and immediately returned to service. Furthermore, the substantial trade involved in paying crews and provisioning the rum-runners meant employment and money in the bank for basic local economic enterprises such as shipbuilding. In short, excessive harassment, heavy fines, and/or jail sentences were not considered to be in anyone's best interests.

The fight against demon rum was anything but simple. In many respects it was a game played between politicians (federal as well as provincial), various enforcement agencies, and the rum-runners. After all, by this time the Roaring Twenties were well underway. As Donald Canney sums it up in *Rum War*: "Much of 'the fuel' that made the roar in 'the roaring 20s' was alcohol – beer, wine, bathtub gin, 'hooch', 'fresh off the boat' – and all of it manufactured, imported, transported, sold, and consumed illegally." For many, it would be a time of glittering prosperity, and on balance, a grand way to forget the miseries of the Great War. As it turns out, the story of rum-running is book-ended by the two world wars. Only the echoes endure.

The Banana Fleet

700 cases Dougherty Pints
280 cases Lincoln Inn Pints
250 cases Golden Wedding Pints
100 cases Lincoln Quarts
50 cases Ambassador Quarts
15 cases Glenmore Pints 40
25 cases Noilly Pints
150 cases Four Aces Pints
10 cases Peter Pan Quarts
75 cases Weston reputed Quarts
175 cases William Penn Pints
100 cases Imperial Weston Quarts

225 cases Old Crow Pints
675 cases Guggenheim Pints
100 cases Jesse Moore Pints
100 cases Peter Pan Pints
50 cases Deluxe Bourbon Pints
Robbie Burns reputed Quarts
15 cases Blue Grass Pints
25 cases Early Times Quarts
200 cases Pikeville Pints
10 cases Deluxe Bourbon Quarts
100 cases Stewart Rye Pints

– List of cargo on *Reo II*'s second last trip, early 1938

In 1923, lured by the higher wages in the rum trade, and rumours of a bonus on each successful trip, Winfred signed on as mate on the *Alcala*, a knockabout schooner captained by Roly Knickle.[1] Along with ten other Banana Fleet boats, *Alcala* was built in Nova

1 As captain of *Andrava* during the gale of August 24, 1927, Knickle and his crew survived a bumpy ride across Sable Island, later shovelling sand from the deck and donating a bottle of it to the Fisheries Museum of the Atlantic in Lunenburg. According to Lohnes in *Captains of Lunenburg County*, "While *Andrava* was battling the storm off the banks huge swarms of fireflies flew above the ship, the presence of which cannot be accounted for."

Some of the Banana Fleet tied up at Riverport, ca. 1938. (Photograph by Gilbert Kempton)

Scotia. Early in her career she served as a salt-banker. But she was a fine sailer, and provided stiff competition for the likes of *Bluenose* and *Delawana* in the 1921 elimination races to determine the challenger for the International Fisherman's Trophy.

Typically, a visit to St. Pierre in the early 1920s would see local labourers load *Alcala* with about 6,000 cases of whisky, fine liquors, and champagne destined for the American market. Loading was always supervised by a supercargo – the term used for cargo superintendent – invariably a well-dressed American who looked after all expenses but who had nothing whatever to do with the ship's operation. Later, after reaching Rum Row, *Alcala* anchored well beyond the territorial limit at a pre-arranged location, awaiting contact boats. All her drops were completed successfully – no hijackings[1] occurred, nor threats of ramming by overzealous USCG cutter captains. For his ability and his general conduct as mate on board *Alcala* in 1925, Winfred is rated "very good" on his Continuous

1 Hijackings of becalmed schooners by land-based pirates became less common in the mid-1920s as motorized boats became available.

Certificate of Discharge by Charles Donovan, himself a rum-runner of considerable repute, Master at the Shipping Office in Yarmouth.

While on *Alcala,* the most exciting incident Winfred recalled occurred on one of his last trips. This involved a run ashore to Bethesda Hospital, New York, aboard a speedboat to receive medical attention for blood poisoning in his little finger following a minor incident on board ship. The trouble originated in a contest among crew members to determine who could support the ship's bell for the longest time using only his little finger. Among macho males at the time, the practice may have owed its popularity to the well-known exploits of French-Canadian strongman Louis Cyr, for whom the one-finger lift was a specialty. *Alcala*'s bell, if brass and seventeen-and-a-half inches in diameter, would have weighed 125 pounds. More likely it was twelve inches in diameter and weighed substantially less, but still on the heavy side. Winfred evidently lost that particular contest as well as his little finger (by amputation) on his left hand. A similar fight at a later date may account for the permanently deformed little finger on his right hand, although the instrument responsible for that injury is not known.

In any event, attracted by the speedboat's departure from *Alcala,* a Coast Guard cutter promptly gave chase. A hail of bullets flew around and all about the speedboat while Winfred sat on deck, helpless, in pain, uncaring really whether he lived or died. Much like being seasick, one might suppose. At last, safe on shore, he spent an entire month at Bethesda Hospital at the syndicate's expense, where he once again used his convalescence as an opportunity to study the laws of the sea. Payment of his bill was made by a generous gift of contraband liquor. Such was the power and the sophistication of his wealthy backers that a socialized medical plan – even had there been one – was not needed.

Shortly following his recovery, Winfred met the exam requirements for his Certificate of Competence and graduated to motorized craft. By this time, in 1925, the Banana Fleet was operating full-time, mainly out of Liverpool and Riverport. Owned by an

American syndicate, it consisted of twelve ships by the late 1920s, eleven of which – all Nova Scotia-built – were modified after the shape of World War I sub-chasers. Narrow, low-slung, and with a flattened bottom, their profile was likened to that of a banana.[1]

With their new-found sea power, these motorized banana-shaped craft would, on occasion, venture to run their loads directly in ashore by the dark of the moon. For this purpose they might download directly from a larger mother ship outside the territorial limit. Winfred tells of one such drop (although he does not name the boat, he hinted broadly that it might have been *Alpaca,* his first command) along the coast of New Bedford, Massachussetts:

Most of the time the speedboats would come right off to us and load up. But sometimes we'd land liquor right on the beach. Every once in a while we would run some right into a harbour or beach. One time we went in with 1,000 cases. We had a pilot on board so he'd know exactly where to take us. So we went in there, and the pilot, he got us a little off course. He took us in, but he took us in too close to the shore. The tide was falling and she started to list over pretty badly, and so we had to climb around the deck using ropes. But we got it ashore and put it in the building.

That was in the nighttime and we had a long time to wait for the tide to come up again – had to wait until 9 or 10 o'clock next morning to get off. Anyway, we were pretty sure we would be caught. Some cutter would be sure and see us there in broad daylight. So we had the wireless set taken ashore. And in the morning you could hear the wild geese calling, honking somewhere up in a lake. And we had all this booze in one building. But I think the fellows ashore had the Customs fixed – a little bribe so they wouldn't know we were coming in – a good bribe. Anyway, it was the finest kind of day. And we made for the limit as fast as we could go. Twelve miles, and we got outside all right. That was a close call – close to New Bedford that was – right by the river.

---

1 On the west coast of Canada their counterpart, the Whiskito Fleet, consisted of converted halibut boats that fed a host of speedy small Moskito contact craft.

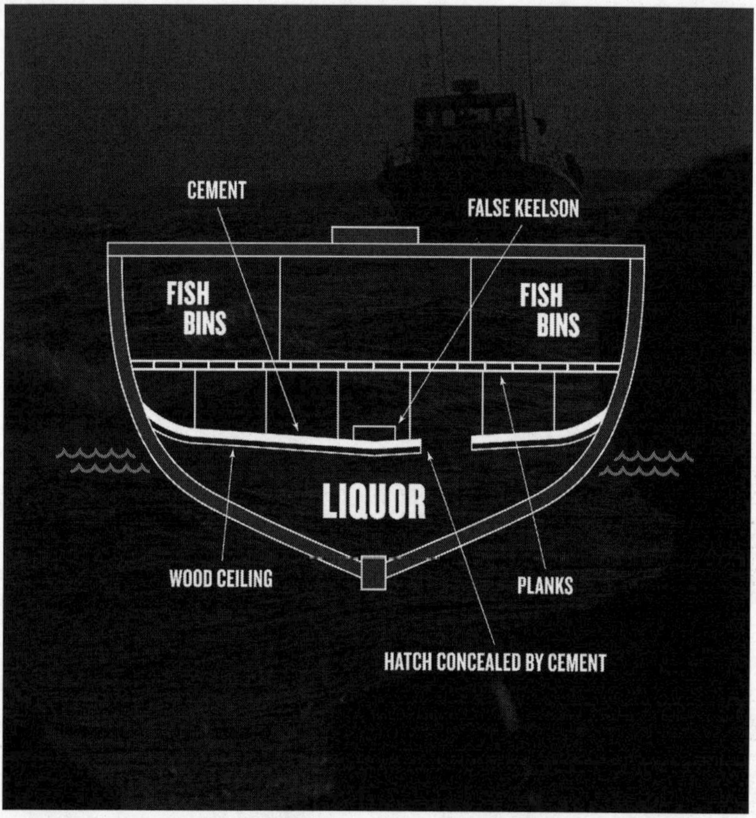

Generalized cross-section of a rum-runner shows how contraband was commonly concealed. (Courtesy of Rum Runners Cake Factory, Halifax)

In *It Came by the Boat Load,* Geoffrey and Dorothy Robinson outline the fate of ten of the Banana Fleet boats, including the *Kilmarnock,* a steel freighter of 160 tons built in England, and thus of completely different construction than her eleven sisters, all of which were built in either Lunenburg or Liverpool. These were *Standard Coaster, Harbour Trader, Ada M., Jacqueline M., Shulamite, Lomergain, Ashtauia, Eleanor Joan,* and *Audrey B.* Although *Marvita* and *Winona R.* are included in the fleet, they were constructed to serve as tankers rather than carry liquor in small containers. *Alpaca* was built in Shelburne, but she also qualifies for membership. Post-Prohibition in the United States, *Reo II* was also considered a member of the club. A good many rum-running vessels bore strange names. For example, the square-sterned *Shulamite* is believed to have been named for a resident of Shunem, a tiny village in ancient Palestine (identified with the modern village of Sulam) that appears in the Song of Solomon.

In all the Banana Fleet boats, a low wheelhouse was located amidships to help avoid detection by the Coast Guard. A popular design, it was widely adopted in the 1930s with the result that motorized rum-runners were difficult to distinguish from each other. Furthermore, it was a common practice to change boats' names at sea, making it difficult for authorities to identify them. Some of the names, as well as the name changes, were intended to be unrecognizable. They also posed a ridiculous challenge to pronounce: examples being *Abracadabra* (or *Abacadaba*), *Etchipotchi, Popacatapelt* (or *Popacatapult*) and *Oui Oui.* Winfred had no trouble with the *Reo II,* but he could never manage to get his tongue around *Maskinoque* (another of the ships he captained from time to time) and was seldom heard to pronounce it the same way twice.

Of all the boats Winfred sailed on as a rum-runner, *Alpaca* was one of the easiest to pronounce. It was not only his first command, it was probably his favourite. His father John Solomon was among the local fishermen who invested hard-earned money in *Alpaca.* Built by master shipbuilder James H. Harding, of Shelburne Shipbuilders Ltd., at a cost of about $25,000, *Alpaca* came off the stocks on November 2, 1927. As shown in USCG photographs preserved in the U.S. National Archives, her superstructure would undergo several changes during her long career.

Alpaca? Well, there's nothing mysterious about the name; curious perhaps, but not mysterious. Not unless you work for the USCG. Ellen Lawson, in her book *Smugglers, Bootleggers, and Scofflaws,* notes that U.S. authorities, ever on the alert but forever

Alpaca is shown here on the stocks, under construction, in Shelburne Shipbuilders yard, 1927. (Courtesy of the Shelburne County Archives and Genealogical Society)

frustrated in their efforts to nab *Alpaca* inside American waters, interpreted the name as "Al packed it" in reference to Al Capone, the kingpin of American crime. Capone was a major figure in Chicago's gang world, as influential in politics as in the world of liquor smuggling, prostitution, and gambling throughout the rum-running era.

It's just possible that Al might have known about *Alpaca,* for he kept in touch with his suppliers. His vested interests in Maritime rum-running were as real as his several nights hotel booking in St. Pierre and his straw hat (on display to this day in Hotel Robert), which he presented to a shopkeeper during a visit to the island in the late 1920s. Jean Andrieux notes in *Rumrunners* that during his visit, Capone recommended the liquor bottles be covered with straw and packed in jute bags to help prevent breakage and to reduce the noise of handling the contraband at sea and the risk of attracting the attention of vigilant cutters. Whether he or Bill McCoy, the famous American rum-runner (one of the first in the business), is credited with this invention is perhaps a moot point. But the practice caught on, and served some very useful purposes, at least from a rum-runner's perspective. In any event, there are compelling indications that a great deal of rum smuggled by Maritime ships reached Al Capone.

Although in his time, Al Capone employed lots of gunslingers, guns on Canadian rum-runners were few, except those packed by the supercargoes. However, on USCG cutters, as on American rum-runners, guns were common. Curiously, one of the great fears among Canadian Maritime rum-runners was that a bullet striking a barrel of rum would cause an explosion. Hugh Corkum's cautionary tale in *On Both Sides of the Law* admonishes that "A sky ride on a keg of rum is not the best way to enter heaven." This scenario may rest in the realm of myth. Several myth-busting television programs (e.g., *The Breaking Point, #4 Gasoline Tanker*) demonstrate that even a container of gasoline does not explode or ignite upon impact with a high-powered rifle shot.[1] The explanation, of course, lies in the fact that ignition requires the presence of oxygen in the mix.

Like his early mentors Norman Conrad and Byron Ritcey, Winfred became a successful rum-runner. Like Norman, although he did not especially work the ships of the Banana Fleet, he sailed on several. By 1931, Byron Ritcey served as shore captain of the fleet, in charge overall, and supervising every vessel on its initial run. Byron was known to his backers as commodore of the fleet. Having captained the *Ada M.* on trips to Rum Row during the early days of rum-running, he was considered an experienced man. And his time spent in a New Jersey jail would seem to prove it.

His sojourn there began in late March 1930, as captain of the

---

1 My son Alexander, an explosives expert, offers – for a small consideration – to stand beside a drum of gasoline targeted by a high-powered rifle shot, provided that the shooter is an experienced and expert marksman, and that the container is full of gasoline and not a mixture of air and gasoline.

Ada M., during the early days of the Banana Fleet. According to a newspaper report, his ship was captured "with 5,000 cases of liquor bottled in quarts, which had been fitted into tins bearing olive oil, crushed fruit and food labels." The liquor was worth an estimated $225,000. Bail was fixed at $5,000 each for the captain and the supercargo, plus $1,500 each for the nine other crew members. Among the crew was deckhand Paul Hirtle, brother to Florence who, forty-two years later, was destined to become Winfred's third wife.

Al Capone's Namesake – Alpaca

While the $23 case goods advance to $45 "over the rail," in the bootlegger's hands, they advance still more rapidly in terms of dollars, for the bootlegger splits his case of Scotch into 24 bottles by simply adding water and alcohol so that the percentage of spirits and taste remains the same in 24 quarts which have grown from 12. The bootlegger makes use of old bottles which contained Scotch before, and the venerable and battered label grows more seemingly with age and servitude. And these "split" goods sell at from $80 a case upwards.

To the exclusive clubs of those who can afford the prices, the bootlegger sells his smuggled Scotch at $110 a case, and in such instances the purchaser gets exactly what he pays for. The steward of the club comes in for his share in the business by charging the bootlegger 50c a bottle for the "empties," corks and labelled caps, which he had steamed off carefully before the bottle was set on the clubman's table. [1]

– "The Bootleggers, Bad Ways and Big Profits"
Progress Enterprise, Lunenburg, January 10, 1923

1 Hugh Corkum in *On Both Sides of the Law* says they kept a suitcase full of labels of the best whisky for the bootleggers.

Winfred's career as a rum-runner spanned nearly fifteen years between 1923 and 1938. Much of this time, especially in the early 1930s, was spent as either captain or mate of the *Alpaca*. Service on a diesel ship was essential in order for a captain to obtain a master's ticket, and in 1936 Winfred was awarded a Certificate of Service as Master "of a steamship ... in the Home Trade ... not exceeding one hundred and fifty tons" by the Minister of Transport, the remarkable C.D. Howe.[1]

Alpaca proved a busy and successful boat, active over a long stretch of the Atlantic seaboard. Well over one hundred locations are marked (with x's) along the three- and twelve-mile offshore limits on a marine chart of a 600-mile-long stretch (as the seagull flies) of coastline reaching from Barnegat Bay, New Jersey, to Annapolis Royal, Nova Scotia. This extraordinary artefact, used by *Alpaca*'s long-serving Captain Winfred Spindler, was donated to the Fisheries Museum of the Atlantic, Lunenburg, by his youngest son, Jack. Its very survival is testament to the fact that *Alpaca* was never seized, for in such an event, documents of this sort were chief among incriminating evidence, and consequently the first to be tossed over the side.

What's in a map? A scrap of paper with an unpretentious scrawl of unsmiling ragged lines, born of a draftsman's measured care. Unlike the pages of a book, this document permits no doubt for the educated eye to dwell upon. The coastline, those islands, and those reefs are real, immovable grid-defined entities. They can, and often do, exact a toll on the ill-informed or careless user. For without a map, a skipper soon realizes that he really is at sea. A good boat in the open ocean is helpful too.

Many rum-runners (e.g., *Shulamite, Lomergain, Standard Coaster, Shanalian, Ganeff, Audrey B., Ada M.,* and *Jacqueline M.*), were hastily constructed using improperly cured wood. However, instead

---

1 A powerful and talented cabinet minister representing the Liberal Party, Clarence Decatur Howe was, in the latter part of his political career, nicknamed "Minister of Everything."

of green softwood, high-quality cured oak, three-inch deck planking, and solid oak railings went into *Alpaca*'s construction. This served the lives of her captain and crews especially well during their trips to various rum rows during her long career.

Alpaca's registry number 153341 gives her statistics as follows: square-stern, 82.8 feet long (on the small side really for a banana boat), beam 18.5 feet, depth 9.9 feet, speed 13 knots, Fairbanks Morse engine of 180 hp., registered tonnage[1] 45.97 – overall in keeping with standards, although no two boats of the Banana Fleet were of the same design. Her carrying capacity was only about half that of *Reo II* (registered tonnage of 87.64), which Winfred captained during the mid-1930s. It is worth noting that on board *Alpaca,* in addition to the usual navigational aids, provision was made for creating smokescreens on demand. A tank filled with oil could be opened to allow the oil to run into the manifold exhaust, instantly producing a dense smoke. The intention was that the smoke, being quite heavy, would hang low over the water, obscuring the boat from revenue ships, whether by day or by night. Best results were evidently obtained under windy conditions.

In Lunenburg, the Fisheries Museum of the Atlantic's exhibit on *Reo II* (unfortunately now minus the boat, which was deemed unrepairable and scuttled in 1985) illustrates life and times during the rum-running era, including a glimpse of Winfred's role. But *Alpaca* was his main command, intermittent though it was, due to the practice of changing captains often. The Change of Masters, though by no means a complete record, shows that Winfred was on board *Alpaca* in December 1927; on August 21, 1931; January 20, 1932; September 1932; and October 16, 1933. His first mentor in navigation, Norman Conrad, served as captain of *Alpaca* just before Winfred succeeded in command. However, Maxwell Lohnes records in *Captains of Lunenburg County* that Captain Norman Conrad was in

1 Registered tonnage of a vessel consists of the total volume of its interior, measured in tons (units of 100 cubic feet). One gross ton (shipping) is equivalent to 2.83168 cubic metres or 100 cubic feet of permanently enclosed space.

Winfred's two-year-old niece, Carolyn Emily Mossman, was overjoyed to receive the present of a seahorse from her favourite uncle, just back from a trip down south in 1932.

command when "the M.S. *Alpaca,* of B.W.I. [British West Indies] of 94 tons arrived in Riverport ... from the high seas ... on 17 September, 1934, on 18 March, 1935, and when she arrived in Riverport from St. Pierre ... on 25 May, 1935 ... on 9 January, 1936."

Winfred made at least one trip to the Caribbean in the early 1930s (possibly January 1932), probably on *Alpaca,* although there is nothing in the shipping records which proves it. Rather, evidence turns up in a photograph of my sister Carolyn, aged two, happily astride her very own inflatable seahorse. This was an artefact discovered floating in the sea by her Uncle Teddy on the way back from a trip down south. So far as is known, the horse is not believed to have contained any contraband, although all things are possible in love and the rum war. More likely, the horse may have blown off the deck of a passing liner, but here the proof is unfortunately lacking because no one recorded its brand and the steed has long since galumphed its way into toy heaven.

Alpaca is not mentioned in many books dealing with the rum trade, which would likely meet with Captain Spindler's approval. That low level of recognition means they were succeeding very well in avoiding detection and seizure by the U.S. Coast Guard. Nevertheless, the USCG was able, through a range of surveillance methods, to maintain a remarkably accurate account of the activities of this British oil screw (motor vessel). To their chagrin, however, they were never able to seize her inside the American territorial limit. Doubtless, the quality of men at Winfred's side helped a great deal. For example, Calvin Silver from Upper Kingsburg, a veteran Grand Banks schooner captain, sailed as mate on several occasions, and Hugh Corkum, well-versed in short-wave wireless (including the new directional finding techniques, later termed radar), tapped the keys of communication for Winfred on several trips during the 1930s. In all, nine men normally crewed the *Alpaca* – captain, mate, engineer, cook, four able seamen, and, of course, Sparky, the common name for the wireless operator, a key ingredient to any successful operation.

It is astonishing just how much the USCG knew about individual rum-runners and their whereabouts. Consider, for example, the very busy ship *Alpaca*. Nearly three years after repeal of the Volstead Act, *Alpaca* was active throughout the Maritimes and along the New England coast. According to the U.S. National Archives, the USCG documents her whereabouts and activities in surprising detail. For example, September 30, 1934, finds her operating thirty miles east of Cape Cod. Then, during the first week in February 1936, she is reported as having successfully delivered (possibly her last load) "in the Boston Division ... slightly in excess of 1,000 cases of alcohol." The following excerpt from their 1935 record for tracking the movement of the British Oil Screw M.V. *Alpaca* further illustrates the sort of record maintained.

24 May – On 16, 17, 18 and 21 May believed active off Nantucket Island, Mass. On 20 May was sighted by Coast Guard plane 131 in position about 30 miles N. x E. off Nantucket Island, Mass.

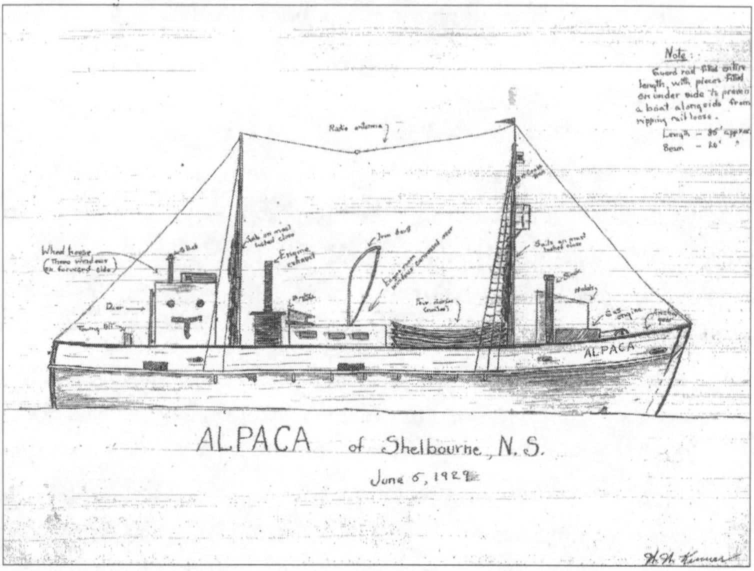

A sketch of *Alpaca* dated June 6, 1929, on file with the United States Coast Guard. Detailed notations include: guardrail fitted entire length with pieces fitted on underside to prevent a boat alongside from ripping rail loose; length 86' approx.; width 20' approx.; wheelhouse – there are 3 windows on the forward side; door; engine room windows closed over; engine exhaust; radio antenna; iron davit; anchor gear; sails on mast lashed close; stack; hatch; booby hatch; 4 dories nested; gas engine; engine exhaust; towing bit. (Courtesy of U.S. National Archives)

31 May – On 24 and 25 May sighted by RCMP Cruiser PREVENTOR and Coast Guard plane about 50 miles southeast of Cape Sable, heading east. On 26 May reported that she entered Riverport, N.S., in ballast. On May 28 cleared Halifax for a Newfoundland port. On May 30 was in the vicinity of HAZEL L. MYRA off Nova Scotia, apparently waiting for a cargo.

7 June – Believed active off the Nova Scotia coast in the vicinity of Cross Island.

14 June – Information indicates that she cleared Lunenburg on the 28th of May for St. John's, Newfoundland. She was expected to receive cargo from HAZEL L. MYRA and may be active off the Nova Scotia coast.

21 June – It is believed that she was active on the 14th and 15th off the coast of Massachusetts, after receiving a cargo from the HAZEL L. MYRA last week. Upon being sighted by Coast Guard plane 131 on 16 June in position about 10 miles S.E. of Pollock Rip Lightvessel [Massachusetts] she appeared to be lighter in the water than on the previous day when observed by plane, thus giving strength to the belief that she made contact with the American Speedboat HOBO on the 16th, the HOBO being seized later on that day at the entrance to Nantucket, Mass., after allegedly jettisoning her cargo. On the 16th she was under trail by the patrol boat ARGO, in position 58 miles northeast of Nantucket Lightvessel and trail continued on the 17th, 18th and 19th to the vicinity of Cross Island, Nova Scotia. Picketed by ARGO in vicinity of Lurcher Shoal Lightvessel. Information indicates she was ordered to meet the LASIRENE in the vicinity of Cross Island; transfer her cargo; and then proceed to Riverport, Nova Scotia.

Although far from being as efficient as the current informational cloud, the efficiency of the USCG's nearly century-old surveillance protocol – spies, interception of radio communications, image gathering, and tapping into public sources – was remarkably good. Conversely, the success enjoyed by *Alpaca* deserves kudos, for despite the intensive efforts to track and predict her movements, she was never seized.

"Say your prayers, boys!"

Badges? We ain't got no badges! We don't need no badges! I don't need to show you any stinking badges.

– Gold Hat (Alfonzo Bedoya) in
Treasure of the Sierra Madre

The sad fact is that few rum-runners – captains or otherwise – left written accounts of their activities. Tape recordings made long after Prohibition ended reveal a hesitancy to name people, places, and dates. A classic illustration goes back to Winfred's early days as a crewman on *Alcala*. A shipmate, he said, was observed to be in a very depressed state for over a week, saying little if anything to anyone. During the homeward trip, while standing watch with his shipmate, Winfred was relieved at the wheel for a short interval late one fine evening. Upon his return, much to his surprise, he found no one at the helm. The call "Man overboard!" roused the entire ship's company. "He must have jumped overboard," said Winfred, adding, "and he was a man who lived not two miles from here." But he would not reveal the name. That matter aside, the stigma surrounding suicide then made it a subject to be avoided. Church policy in some instances forbade burial of a suicide within a communal plot.

The traditional three-mile territorial offshore limit was extended to twelve miles in 1924. According to Donald Canney in *Rum War,* the USCG began their great offensive in May 1925. Harassment was ramped up and longer patrols were initiated. Yet even with the addition of twenty-five destroyers – most of them four-stackers left over from World War I – to patrol Rum Row, the amount of contraband liquor making it ashore continued to increase. Like the destroyers, USCG cutters, ranging from 70 to over 100 feet long, were well armed and, given their mood and their mandate, they did not hesitate to deploy their firepower.

Captain William Cluett of Lunenburg, on the *Josephine K.*, was killed by cannon fire from a USCG cutter in 1931. A year or so earlier Winfred had sailed on that ship with him. Although no mention was ever made of his time on board, Winfred readily admitted to having routinely come under fire from the Preventive Services. In the late 1930s, *Josephine K.* would be one of the first rum-runners sold for service on Prince Edward Island, reportedly still bearing the marks of shellfire on her hull. The practice of ramming the enemy was fairly common too, with at least one aggressive cutter captain making it his specialty. One example is the sinking of the *Symore* by the 125-foot-long cutter *Legare* off Nantucket Lightship in the spring of 1931, according to *Symore*'s captain Aubrey Backman of Riverport. But there were several other rum-runners sunk in this manner in the vicinity of the forty- to sixty-mile zone of the American coast.

Winfred admits that, while he was in command of *Alpaca,* USCG cutters rammed it on two occasions. On one occasion a 75-foot-long cutter[1], roughly equal to *Alpaca* in length, and probably also in speed, rammed them without causing serious damage. The other instance involved the *Fanning,* a destroyer, a four-stacker. This is about as close as Winfred ever came to boasting. Leaving much

1 Personnel at the National Archives, Washington, D.C., advise they have no knowledge of any collision between *Alpaca* and any of the smaller USCG cutters.

Alpaca at speed, ca. 1934. (Courtesy of the Fisheries Museum of the Atlantic, Lunenburg)

unsaid, he'd only add, "They thought they'd sunk *Alpaca*."

USCG destroyers were large, well-armed, powerful ships. Burning oil and using steam turbines for propulsion they were capable of speeds in excess of 30 knots (35 mph, 56 km/hr). Malcolm Willoughby in *Rum War at Sea* states *Fanning*'s tonnage as 742, and overall length 293 feet. Some of those four-stackers survived to see service in World War II. Their task along Rum Row was to shadow rum-runners, especially the mother ships as they hovered to unload, and to seize contact boats seeking to deliver liquor to shore destinations. In many cases, a threatened collision initiated during this energy-intensive game of chance morphed into a deliberate game of chicken, by either one or both participants. The Robinsons pretty well sum it up in *It Came by the Boat Load* when they explain that a slight miscalculation sometimes meant that "instead of just missing, they just hit." As a case in point, take the archived account of the collision off the coast of New England of *Alpaca* with the USS *Fanning,* captained by LCDR Norman Henry Leslie, on the evening of Friday, February 27, 1930.

The four-stacker, *CG-11 Fanning* of the U.S. Coast Guard docked alongside a second destroyer ca. 1930. (From official Coast Guard website, courtesy of the U.S. National Archives)

Alpaca had been tagged by a small (125-foot-long) USCG cutter almost upon arrival on Rum Row off New London, Connecticut, a week earlier. For several days and nights, as a storm developed, the cutter shadowed *Alpaca* in cat-and-mouse tactics familiar to all hands on both sides. Each ship had a challenging job at the best of times, and never more so than under poor weather conditions. Thanks to the heavy weather, the cutter gave it up as a bad job on the morning of February 27 and headed to safety ashore. *Alpaca* had no choice but to stay and face the elements.

Just after the cutter departed mid-morning on the 27th, the monster four-stacker, USS *Fanning CG-11* showed up. Despite the ominous threat of this fresh picket, patience on *Alpaca* was wearing thin. Watchmen on the *Fanning* seemed especially diligent, constantly keeping *Alpaca* in view, watching for any new maneuver by their prey. Most annoying to men on the *Alpaca* were the two powerful searchlights mounted either side of the *Fanning*'s bridge, one or the other of which – and sometimes both – beamed upon them constantly as early night set in. They prayed for even worse weather

– a good thick fog, or heavy snow, anything that might create a realistic escape window for them. Deep in the water with a full load of 2,500 cases, *Alpaca* had already been waiting about fifty miles southeast of the eastern tip of Long Island for nearly a week for a chance to call out the contact boats. And that was where *Fanning* tagged her. On board *Alpaca* the feeling was that action was overdue; anything to break the boring, ceaseless picketing.

At 5:45 p.m., *Alpaca* was running fast, downwind some 400 yards or so, ahead of her pursuer. She'd made various maneuvers during the last hour, despite high seas, to try and escape her tag – running circles around the destroyer, going flat out in different directions, then pulling the tail of the cat by keeping close to the stern of the big ship while its captain did his utmost to anticipate *Alpaca*'s next move. This in no way amounted to a trivial pursuit in the eyes of Captain Leslie on board the *Fanning*. His job was certainly made no easier as night fell, even with spotlights. Now, in the dark of early evening, the annoying bright carbon-arc light played relentlessly upon the *Alpaca*.

"Look a' here, Skipper, this is gettin' some tiresome! Tonight's the night, we got to shake this bugger once and for all," says the mate, Calvin Silver. "He can see we're loaded and there's no way he's leaving."

"OK, we've been leading them on for quite a while now," says Captain Winfred Spindler. "Get ready to pour on the smoke as we head into the wind. We'll try a quick turn. Douse all lights."

"It's worth a try," the mate responds.

Completing her 180-degree turn at high speed, *Alpaca* took a terrific hammering. No sooner done than dense black smoke billowed from *Alpaca*'s exhaust downwind against the four-stacker. On board the hunted, hope soared as *Alpaca* was enveloped in darkness. Steadied now on the reverse of her previous course, she swiftly increased the distance between the two ships. Or at least she thought she did.

Things were looking pretty good for a few minutes, as *Alpaca* drove on through the night. But her escape was momentary. Suddenly the spell was broken as the searchlights found them again. Somehow, the four-stacker had tracked their path along the smoky trail upwind. A thin snow squall blew past, chasing the remains of the smokescreen, but it contributed nothing to hiding them from the tag. Again, the deck of *Alpaca* was lit up, bright as day.

"Goddamn it all! Now what?"

"Hang on, and we'll try going backwards for a spell. Maybe we can scare her off," jokes Winfred. "I'm taking her full astern."

On board the *Fanning* consternation reigned. Too late they discovered *Alpaca*'s desperately deliberate maneuver. A bow-to-stern collision loomed large. The four-stacker's speed fell off slowly as her screws worked furiously in reverse to slow the giant. It would have been a close thing, except that one of the ships veered at the last moment such that they were only a few feet apart as they slowly passed each other. By the wheelhouse of the 82-foot-long *Alpaca* – a cockle shell compared to the vastly heavier 293-foot-long *Fanning* – the watch could only look in despair at the glistening cliff of steel slipping by.

"God Almighty, she's turning into us," someone yelled. "This is it! Say your prayers, boys!"

Time slowed to nothing as the sharp bow of the four-stacker rounded in slow motion on *Alpaca* and ground into her side, bending "the stem of the *Fanning* to starboard ... at about the ten foot draft mark," or so said the complaining dispatch about "Official Number 153,341" sent to the American Acting Minister of Marine, E. Hawken, on June 13, 1930. But those were about the only facts agreed upon in the unresolved dispute which followed between Ottawa and the U.S. Chargé d'Affaires B. Reath Riggs.

For their part, *Alpaca*'s crew would never forget that sickening lurch, which drove the boat on her beam ends for what seemed like an eternity. But they did recall the piercing whistle blast of the four-stacker just after they struck. And then, glory be to all that's holy, *Alpaca* somehow righted herself, and plunged away, still in reverse.

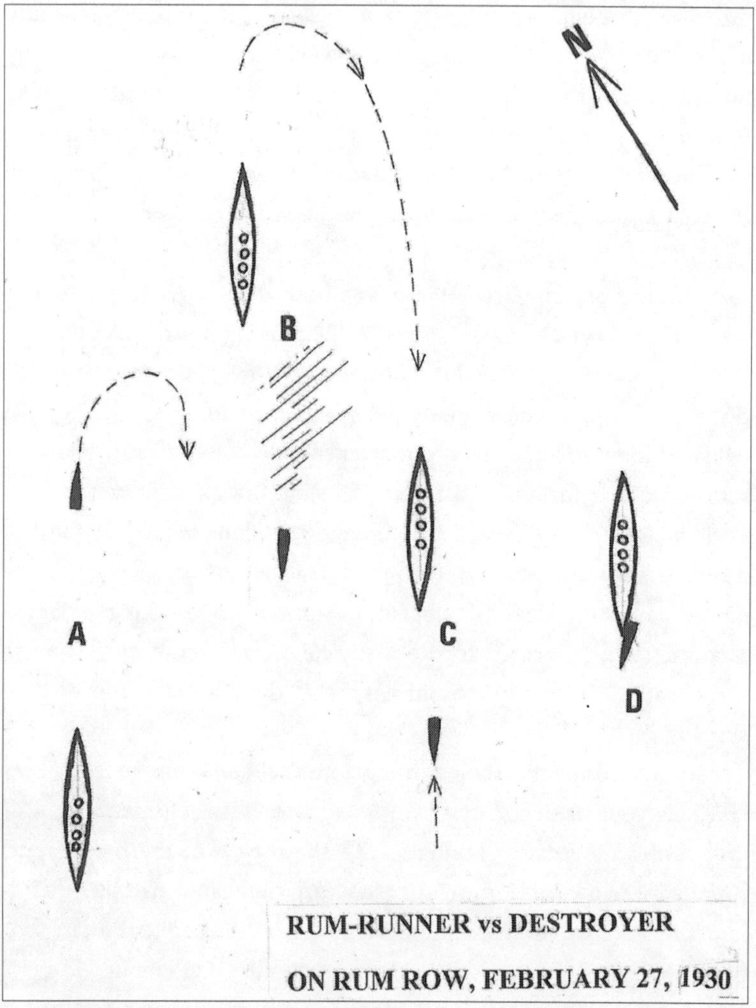

February 27, 1930. (A) 5:45 p.m. Pursued by *Fanning*, *Alpaca* turns suddenly through 180 degrees. (B) 5:47 p.m. *Fanning* turns to follow *Alpaca*. (C) 5:55 p.m. Discovered through her smokescreen, *Alpaca* reverses direction, heading backwards towards *Fanning*, which also throws her engines into reverse. (D) 5:57 p.m. Ships converge and collide.

"By God, that was a close one. Good thing we've got lots of ballast," Winfred laughs as the crew assembles for a head count after a hasty check reveals that *Alpaca* remains fully operational. He was seldom at a loss for quick and efficient rapport when it came to cutting to the core of crisis. "Surprisingly little damage," he adds cheerfully. "Old Harding did a good job on this one." Then, moments later, as a boat puts off from the destroyer's side toward *Alpaca*, "Looks like visitors coming. Prepare to help them on board. This should be just a formality."

And it was. Since the "accident" took place well outside the territorial limit, there was little the Coast Guard could do except register protest. This formality was duly accomplished by proponents on both sides in the argument. However, *Alpaca* could be said to have enjoyed a distinct advantage, playing host to the boarding party. And she was still afloat. The disgruntled boarding party from *Fanning* made their way back to the destroyer. It seems that she had suddenly developed a significant leak. A little while later, *Fanning* made off into the night, directly for port in New London.

"Seems like our friend has a bloody nose and has to go home. Now, isn't that too bad! Maybe that will teach him not to harass us outside the limit," mutters the mate Calvin Silver to no one in particular.

"Hello, Sparky, see if you can raise our contact and set up a good site for offloading. Just keep it in code. We don't want any more trouble. If our luck holds we'll be headed home in a day or so," says Winfred. "And now, I think we could all use a drink."

Extracts from the Commanding Officer's Cruise Report, dated February 28, 1930, supply a slightly different account of the incident.

At daybreak, 26th February, scouted southward on rectangular courses from Cox Ledge. Anchored in the Sakonnet River at dark on account of heavy weather offshore and northeast storm warnings received.

Proceeded at daybreak 27th February and scouted southward from the Sakonnet River. At 0952, in Latitude 40'–41' N, Longitude

71'–13' W, identified the SILVER ARROW of Lunenburg, N.S. At about the same time, sighted two other suspicious looking vessels to the southeastward and proceeded in that direction. At 1030, identified and stopped to picket the ALPACA of Shelbourne, N.S. in Latitude 40'–33' N., Longitude 71'–00' W. The SILVER ARROW and the other ship sighted soon disappeared over the horizon to the eastward. At 1800, in Latitude 40'–33' N., Longitude 71'–00'W., with the ALPACA abeam off FANNING'S port bow, headed in the opposite direction, ALPACA suddenly turned to port going at considerable speed and struck the FANNING on the port side of the stem, fracturing the bow plating and bending the stem to starboard at the waterline. Sent officer on board the ALPACA to exchange usual information. While boat was returning, ALPACA doused all lights and was lost. Set course for New London at reduced speed.

By 2 a.m. on Saturday, February 28, *Fanning* was safely moored at State Pier, New London, Connecticut. Hard as it may seem to credit, the four-stacker came off far worse than *Alpaca* in the collision. According to his letter of March 4, 1930, the Commander, Destroyer Force, advised the Commandant of the Coast Guard that, "As a result of the collision, her stem and bow plating were badly twisted," and "the cost of repairs will amount to $2,500." He added, "It will also be necessary to renew two sections of main steam-piping to backing turbine, starboard side at a cost of $500."

Damage to *Fanning*'s bow was so severe that she made for shore directly, before determining for certain whether *Alpaca* would be lost (i.e., sunk) as a consequence of damage sustained, or could make way under her own steam. However, despite the violent shaking inflicted by her predator, *Alpaca* – more of a workhorse than her diminutive name might suggest – continued on to deliver her goods and returned to Yarmouth for minor repairs to her three-inch oak planking and thick oak guardrail. Total cost of that job was $500, in contrast to the $3,000 worth of damage sustained by the *Fanning*.

Adding insult to injury, the sworn statement by the Master of

Alpaca before the Collector of National Revenue at Yarmouth was duly forwarded to the Secretary of State in Washington, D.C. In his letter accompanying the sworn statement, the U.S. Chargé d'Affaires comments, "As might be expected, the Master of the *Alpaca* denies his responsibility for any damage to the *Fanning*."

For the record, *Alpaca*'s captain denied pretty well everything. Excerpts from Captain Winfred Spindler's letter, sworn before M.C. Wyman, Collector of National Revenue in Yarmouth on June 17, 1930, read as follows:

I, Winfred Oswald Spindler, Master of the ship or vessel called ALPACA, registered at Shelburne, in the Province of Nova Scotia, Dominion of Canada, Official Number 153,341, registered tonnage 45.97, make oath and state that August 19th, 1929, I was placed in command of the vessel ALPACA and have been Master of this vessel up to the present date.

... under oath I make the solemn declarations to the information as contained in the above dispatch referred to:

That on or about 6 P.M. the latter part of February, 1930, the date 27th February, 1930, I am not sure about, the FANNING was in collision with the British oil screw ALPACA.

That I have no knowledge at the time of the collision, the engines of the FANNING were making full speed astern, the ship being practically dead in the water.

That the FANNING was steering different courses as well as the ALPACA when they met at this occasion.

I deny the fact as stated, that when ahead of the bow of the FANNING the ALPACA suddenly changed course, heading directly across the bow of the FANNING.

That the Officer of the Deck of the FANNING made an attempt to sound the danger signal but that the collision occurred before one blast had been sounded on the whistle.

That the point of impact was on the port bow, hitting the stem about the ten foot draft mark.

That the forward part of the ALPACA and her guard rail came in contact with the stem.

That the stem of the FANNING was bent to starboard, but the extent of the bend I have no knowledge of.

I cannot state that the proper lookouts were stationed on the bridge of the FANNING.

I deny that I am responsible as Master of the ALPACA at the time of the collision with the FANNING for any damage which occurred.

That at the time of the collision the running lights of both ships were burning, and that I do not remember making a statement to the effect that the ALPACA was being run around warming up the engines, but I do state that there was more than one man on deck at the time.

I am not positive that the ALPACA was laden with liquor or in ballast at the time of the collision.

That I do not remember the speed the ALPACA was going at the time of the collision.

That nothing more ever came of this or numerous other similar incidents illustrates the unanswered question expressed in a letter to the Commandant of the United States Coast Guard by Captain Chas. S. Root, Lt. Commander of Coast Guard Intelligence. Specifically, Captain Root sought clarification in this case "concerning the authority of the Empire over shipping and as to whether the British Merchant Shipping Act or the various Dominion statutes are in fact the authoritative law." The problem centred on the questionable right claimed by British ships to transport and to transfer liquor offshore of the United States. There was, of course, no simple, straightforward answer. Commandant Rear Admiral Frederick C. Billard replied he did not have time to study the case, conceding on August 1, 1930, that "It does seem that we ought to at least go on record as having asked [the Department of] Justice to do this."

Several years later, Stanley V. Parker, Chief of the Division of Intelligence, received a welcome update from USCG Intelligence Officer S.S. Yeandle on November 2, 1936, reporting the status of *Alpaca*. As quoted from the Yarmouth *Telegram*, October 16, 1936:

"Her adventurous career as a member of Al Capone's rum-running fleet has ended for the M.V. *Alpaca,* which has been bought [for $8,000] by the Kyuquot Co-operative Fish Company of west coast Vancouver Island, and will be used for carrying fish." Incidentally, the captain for the trip through the Panama Canal and up the west coast to her new owners in British Columbia was Joey Wentzell of Riverport.

Playboy in Rum-Runner Heaven

Rum is a burning mercy, still it's many a young man's joy.
Causes many a loving mother to mourn for her darling boy.

– "Deck of the Willow Green"
Folk Ballads and Songs
of the Lower Labrador Coast
MacEdward Leach

During the 1930s, Winfred was mainly based in Yarmouth, conveniently near the western end of Nova Scotia and the closest point of departure of Banana Fleet boats for Rum Row. Yarmouth, with a population of 7,000, was humming with business. It had pretty well everything – shipyards, repair depots, well-stocked warehouses, accommodating citizens, and a grand hotel. As terminus to the Eastern Steamship Company, it was an extremely busy port. A daily ferry service from Boston or New York fit the needs of syndicate movers and shakers perfectly. They, in turn, were highly appreciative of this small town's politics. In Yarmouth, everyone knew everyone else, a feature which enabled potential spies to be sorted out pretty quickly. The locals tended to be protective of their own.

A few telling photographs and fragments of oral history indicate that, in his prime, Winfred had a taste for women and fast

Winfred, at the wheel of his 1929 Oldsmobile, and an unidentified friend, in a scene reminiscent of *Bonnie and Clyde*.

cars. No surprise there. He may have worked hard, but he was making big money, so he played hard too. Though perhaps inclined to parsimony in later years, he was with good reason untouched by it at this stage in life. Payoffs in the $1,000 range were made in Yarmouth at the end of each successful trip, and Winfred made a lot of them. The price of a car in those days was about six to seven hundred dollars. A top-of-the-line Chrysler coupe with wire wheels cost less than $1,500.

Winfred owned a succession of cars during his years as a rumrunner, and it could be said that he had a heavy foot. While at the time there may not have been a whole lot of pavement available upon which to peel rubber, he did his best to tear up the province's dirt roads. No question, Winfred enjoyed his time in Yarmouth between trips to St. Pierre and Rum Row. His term for it was "sporting," though there was doubtless a fair bit of hell-raising along the way. More than once he wrecked a new vehicle. To his parents' dismay, he appeared unconcerned about these write-offs. His mother,

Clara Augusta, was quite put out, to say the least, by her son's wild behaviour. I remember her comments (made out of her son's hearing) concerning Winfred and his cars back in the rum-running days.

"Winfred went through a lot of cars," she told me. "I asked him one morning, seeing that the driveway was empty, 'Where's your car, Winfred?' 'Oh,' was the reply, 'that's down over the bank somewhere.'"

All things considered, it is scarcely surprising that of the seven virtues, Winfred might have leaned towards two of the cardinal four, namely courage (on several obvious accounts) and prudence (given that he was worldly wise and, if anything, excessively discreet). It may be stretching things a bit to include temperance, though he was generally moderate in his consumption of food (with the exception of raw eggs) and drink, despite the cornucopia sometimes on offer. Now and then he enjoyed a good cigar, likewise packing a lip with snuff, but neither practice was carried on to excess. Justice? Well now, from a rum-runner's perspective – and bearing on international law respecting marine jurisdictions – he felt justice was served by tweaking the nose of a four-stacker.

In Yarmouth, in quieter moments, he developed lifelong friends in local businessman Fred Fairn and his family, with whom he boarded. For many years, the men enjoyed each other's company hunting in the fall, after Fred and his family moved to the country northwest of Bridgewater. Winfred loved hunting wildfowl and deer, and was blessed with excellent eyes and a wicked aim to match.

His eyes for the fairer sex at the Yarmouth Hospital School for Nursing doubtless brought about many pleasant encounters. But there was no shortage of women back home in Riverport and District either, as he discovered every month or so, during ritual return trips to his home in Lower Rose Bay.

Winfred enjoyed his freedom as a youthful adventurer. He recalls a brush with the law on one trip home to Riverport in company with a nursing school candidate whose home was in West Dublin.

They caught us twice in Yarmouth, coming in, having booze on board that we shouldn't have had on board. It cost $700 each time. We shouldn't have been caught that often. I'd bring rum home for Christmas, New Year's and everything, all kinds of wine, cigarettes, perfume.

There were a lot of boats that used Yarmouth for headquarters. I got acquainted with a man and his wife – he worked on the boats – and was invited to their house. They seemed pretty nice people. They wanted me to come up and stay with them while in port. So I got a room there for a small amount of money. It was a good place to stay while in port.

Talk about liquor being landed, I'd always bring some in every trip. And I got a little cheeky one trip, so since I hadn't been home for a while I thought I'd bring a few cases home. Make a bit of extra money, you see. Well, the man that I stayed with, he was a hunter, and he gave me some meat. He said, "Do you want some deer meat to bring home?" "Yes," I said, "but I got a lot of other stuff, so I shouldn't take too much." So he gave me ten or fifteen pounds of deer meat – out of season, you – and all the liquor I had, and cigarettes, for the trip down here, home.

If they'd catch me, they'd have had me on about five different charges. I had some guns with me. And I shot a couple of partridges along the way – out of season – and I had my rifle there, and ten or fifteen pounds of deer meat, and wine, and rum, cigarettes, perfume. Anyway, everything was all right until we got close to Liverpool. And I had a nurse with me at the time, from over in West Dublin – a Parks girl – she was a nurse in Yarmouth and she was coming home with me. She was through working for a while.

And we got up to a car on a curve and I went and passed this car on the curve. And I heard this fellow blow all along, and I thought, well, he wants to pass me, so I stepped on it. But the horn kept blowing, so I thought I'd better stop. And I stopped, and this cop came there. And it happened to be a man from across the river, a Ritcey, who was on the police force. He would have known Johnny Mossman, the Prohibition-Revenue Officer in LaHave, and that wouldn't have been so good for me.

Well, he says, do you have a license? Show me your licence. So I pulled that out, and that was all right. Well, he says, don't you think you were going too fast? Well, I didn't deny it. I knew I was going too fast, especially on a curve. So the nurse, she pipes up and says, "He hasn't been home for a while, and he's kind of anxious to get home." I forget all that she told him. Then he opened the back door, and the gun fell out. You see, I had everything piled up there, so he must have known that something was going on. But it could be he knew the nurse's family across in West Dublin there.

Anyway, I had a flag in the back of the window, across, and he says, "Take that flag down." And he says, "Well, I'll let you go this time, but don't let it happen again." And I thanked him, and I felt some good, because I could have lost the car, and the rifle and the shotgun. I would have been a lot of money out. Well, anyways, I got clear of him. I just happened to strike one of the good guys.

Winter Run to Rum Row

Of course, saving life at sea is more or less a habit with sailors, all in the day's work, and nothing to call for remark.

– *Via London* by Archibald MacMechan

With an income well over $1,000 per month, Winfred felt little financial pain throughout the rum-running era. And he enjoyed the adventure. What could be better than making top money doing what you enjoyed? Even so, perils of various sorts hounded the rum-runner at sea. But life at sea is all risk, and an extra one or two in a day's work hardly count for much. However, true of virtually all life experiences, there were certain aspects of the rum trade that Winfred definitely did not enjoy.

He and his crew members would not have been very happy when they lost the cook off the *Alpaca* during one trip. That occasion, undocumented except for a written statement dictated by Winfred to my diarist mother, unfortunately was never elaborated.

But that was life on the high seas. Hazards have a habit of turning up when least expected. Lives can be snuffed out in an instant. Without prompting, Winfred was never one to mention, let alone dwell upon, tragedy; much better to recall happy times and successful outcomes. To hear him tell it:

No, I enjoyed rum-running, but not in winter. Once you left St. Pierre, you had to stay out, no matter what. There was no turning back to port.

Certain parts I did not like at all. Well, in the wintertime, when you left port, you were out. There was no coming in. If there was a gale of wind, or something, you had to take whatever came along. So in the wintertime, when you left home to go to St. Pierre to load up, it would be getting worse down in the east all the time. It would get colder, and sometimes there'd be ice coming out of the gulf, so you'd have to go around Sable Island. And then, when you got loaded with liquor, you had seven hundred miles ahead of you, against the wind much of the time, at four or five miles an hour. It was pretty tough some winters, in February. You had a big mallet to pound the ice. Sometimes you had to stop and pound the ice when the boat, she'd get a big list on. And the windows would freeze up. You couldn't see where you were going. Anyway, that wasn't so good.

We had two men on the watch. Engineer didn't have to stand watch – two engineers – chief and the second engineer. And the cook didn't have to stand watch. And the captain and Sparky didn't stand watch. Sailors and the mate had all the watches. I was mate at the time.

When we left St. Pierre, bound for the American coast, it was blowing a good breeze, not such a bad day. But then, the second day out we got in trouble near Sable Island. We was going along, well, the wind was northerly, and getting pretty cold. I was on watch with another man. And we saw Sparky come up. And he had what you call the toilet ... a wooden bucket[1]*. So he took the risk and stood out on the deck, and did what he had to do. And when he dumped it overboard, he went along with it. So we saw him when he went over. We was going away from him, and the dory was so iced up we couldn't get the dory out. Everything was ice. So we turned the boat around, and came down off the wind and kept watching him. He was there on his back, but he'd kicked his boots off – that was the only thing that saved him.*

1. There was no head (toilet) and no running water on rum-runners.

As mate, it put me on the spot[1]*. I got up in the bow with a big long gaff, about seven foot long. It had a kind of hook on it. And the captain, I told him how to keep, how to steer. The wind was, oh, about fifteen or twenty miles [per hour] – it wasn't rough. We came down as close as we could to him, and kept him on the lee side, so we wouldn't mind the wind so much. So, when we got up to him, I told the captain to come astern on him. And we came astern, right close to him. And I had this gaff, so then it was up to me to make sure that I got him.*

I didn't know if I should put the gaff right into him. I thought I might catch him under the arm with it. Anyway, I got the gaff into him some which way, and kept him close, so he wouldn't get too much water in his lungs. So then we looked around for a piece of rope. But everything was frozen up. But after a while we found a piece of rope, and we got the rope underneath of him, and the gaff. We pulled him up – we didn't heist him – we just pulled him on deck and took him down in the forecastle. He was unconscious.

So I don't know who was the first-aid person, but we knew enough for to roll him around. And we had some brandy, so we poured it down his throat. And when it got down, it started whatever, something. The water was in his lungs and stomach somewhere. And he puked, same as a hose. It came out of him just like a hose. Then we rolled him around some more in the forecastle, just to make sure.

And we wrapped him in all the blankets we could find around. Put lots of heat on him. And after a while he started to come to. And I think he was due for an interview in two hours time. We had a schedule with an American station. But he was all right then, he could tap the keys. He was the [wireless] operator.

If we'd have lost him, we'd have had to go back to St. Pierre, and it would have been an awful mix-up. So we was really lucky to get him. All he lost was a pair of boots and fifteen dollars he had in his pockets. That's all he lost instead of his life.

---

1 Although the ship's captain is ultimately held responsible, the mate is always the go-to guy who answers the call in an emergency.

Death in the Afternoon

Ruin hath taught me thus to ruminate, –
That Time will come and take my love away.
This thought is as a death, which cannot choose
But weep to have that which it fears to lose.

– Sonnet 64, William Shakespeare

It was Tuesday afternoon, May 16, 1933, two days after Mother's Day. The weather was mild, but a strong wind from the northwest drove before it a scattering of light cloud. Left over from stormy conditions a day earlier, the breeze pushed high waves across the LaHave River estuary despite the relatively short fetch. Unfortunately, the tide was high at about noontime. Timing, they say, is everything. Rearing higher in the suddenly shallower water, the waves crashed in surprise against the rocky sea wall beside the road, repeatedly spraying great plumes across it.

Struggling back to the large four-room Riverport School at about one o'clock following lunch at home in the village centre, a small group of grade primary children made their way westward along the roadside towards school. Most of them faced traffic as instructed by their parents – advancing on the left side of the dirt road. But it was a challenge. The temptation was great to cross to the other side and try and dodge the gauntlet of successive wet curtains of spray hurled across the roadway.

From the other direction, a car approached Riverport from Lower LaHave. At the wheel was Winfred Spindler, and with him several friends. They were passing thoroughly familiar landmarks: Riverport School to the right; to the left, a long wharf marked the former location of the old Temperance Hall, which was dismantled several years earlier and moved to LaHave. Winfred glanced toward the school where he noticed several children playing in the yard. They compelled his attention. But he did not see six-year-old Wesley L. Ritcey, son of S. (Samuel) Russell and Mina Ritcey, as the child ran excitedly beneath the airborne remains of a large wave which had burst upon the shore on the opposite side of the road, a stone's throw beyond the schoolyard.

The impact registered on Winfred and the vehicle's occupants as a sudden sense of horror. The cold spectre of grief gripped him by the throat, for as the driver he recognized his culpability in an instant. But there was little anyone could do. The small boy lay completely unresponsive, prone near the centre of the road. As the call went out to summon the doctor, Lawrence Hancock, principal of the school, carefully moved the boy and laid him beside some trees on the landward side of the road in front of Keziah Lohnes's home.

Whether Wesley dodged to the centre of the road at the last instant will never be known. That matters little. "The boy was struck in the head by the mudguard of the car," according to a newspaper report the next day. The pieces of such a jigsaw tale of tragedy are painfully difficult to reconstruct exactly.

Classes were cancelled that afternoon, and an inquest was held later that day at the school, attended by the school trustees, Joshua Backman and Charles Ritcey among them. The coroner's jury later returned a verdict of accidental death. The RCMP investigation reached the same conclusion. Results of an autopsy reported on May 29 by Dr. Geoffrey Barss found the cause of death to be a

Wesley L. Ritcey's sixth birthday party in 1932, in front of Ritcey Brothers store opposite the ice cream parlour, Riverport. From left to right: Wesley, Linda Ritcey (Tolman), George Himmelman, Charlotte Ritcey (Boates), Evelyn Creaser, Doris Creaser, and Erna Creaser. (Photograph courtesy of Charlotte Boates)

fractured skull. Dr. Barss, the local doctor, and a veteran front-line medic during the Great War, was well acquainted with trauma.

It has been said that a large part of you dies with your child. When your parents die, you lose your past. When your husband or wife dies, you lose your present. But when your child dies, you lose your future. Certainly, for Russell and Mina Ritcey, their son's death was a terrible loss. They took it very hard. Wesley was an only son.

Given the absence of formal counselling, Winfred's woes were doubtless compounded by his perception that he was the target of community speculation. All well-being and resolve suddenly counted for naught. Guilt's power to disorient and bewilder took over quickly, and he journeyed through a tunnel of agony in the days and weeks that followed.

In their grief, Russell and Mina's strong religious convictions provided a shaky fallback position. They favoured ostracizing Winfred. Russell, a church elder at a time when eldership was considered an elite position, would long maintain the single adamant vote against Winfred Spindler's admission to membership in Trinity United Church. For Winfred, little therapy would have been available, except perhaps commiseration offered by fellow members in the Independent Order of Odd Fellows, Confidence Lodge No. 106.

Winfred became a very sick man following Wesley's death – sick in heart, mind, and soul. His body retreated to such a shrunken frame that his parents Clara Augusta and John Solomon feared for his life. These deeply religious folk will have wondered as they prayed for their son, and on many Sundays in our church, the popular hymn "Will Your Anchor Hold in the Storms of Life" seemed an utterly appropriate hymn to the times.

In the spring, because their old Cape Cod house was being renovated, Winfred and his parents made their home in one of the family's two fish stores on the shore below the old homestead. Normally dedicated to net-mending and storage of fishing gear, it proved comfortable and roomy enough, for his sisters were away at work and study in New England. It supplied a crucial retreat and a salvation of sorts for Winfred. The early dawn raucous chorus of make-and-break engines, pushing half a dozen or more double-enders out through the harbour channel and across the bar past Rocker Cove toward deep waters, proved irresistible to this born fisherman. A spell of shore fishing with his father gradually strengthened Winfred's will to live. Mid-October of 1933 saw him as captain once more at the helm of *Alpaca*. His anchor appeared to be holding, though it seems fair to suggest that he might never completely recover.

A stained-glass window in Trinity United Church, Rose Bay, dedicated in 1963 by S. Russell Ritcey to his wife Mina, shows Mary and Joseph in the Temple offering their child to God. According to scripture, Simeon, a very righteous and devoted man, took the child in his arms and blessed God. (Photograph courtesy of Subin Upadhyay)

Book 3
Sobering Up

The End of an Era

I wish somehow that we could prohibit the use of alcohol and merely drink beer and whisky and gin as we used to.

– "The Strenuous Age"
Frenzied Fiction
Stephen Leacock

With the repeal of the Volstead Act on April 7, 1933, Prohibition officially ended in the United States, and people were allowed to drink again. In Nova Scotia, of course, it was over and done with already back in 1929. Still, the rum trade, although diminished in volume to Rum Row off the American coast, continued to be worthwhile for the syndicates. Maritime rum-runners gradually increased their focus on the home market. Here, despite the ostensible monopoly on the purchase, transport, distribution, and sale of liquor by the freshly minted (April 31, 1930) Nova Scotia Liquor Commission, a brisk illegal trade endured. Old habits are hard to break. Yet change was underway. In Canada, by the early 1930s the Customs Preventive Service of the Customs and Excise Department was absorbed into the RCMP. After May 1932, the RCMP took over the role of provincial police and was responsible for enforcing all statutes.

But the RCMP was slow to realize that a vast amount of liquor (Demerara rum as well as Canadian liquor originally exported legally to St Pierre) was finding its way back into Canada from St. Pierre, thus evading excise duty. The Preventive Service folks were not impressed. Nor was Conservative Prime Minister R.B. Bennett, who had hounded the previous Liberal Prime Minister Mackenzie King for failing to act on the recommendations of a Royal Commission to prosecute the Bronfman brothers. Convinced at last that a major conspiracy was taking place, paper trails were unravelled and lengthy court actions against suspected rum-runners were initiated against two different establishments. Those trials and the rumblings of a second world war would eventually bring an end to the practice.

Jean Andrieux in *Rumrunners* adeptly documents the role played by the Bronfman brothers in establishing major distillery operations in Ontario and Quebec. The Bronfmans are also alleged to have had interests in smuggling Canadian-produced liquor back into Canada from St. Pierre without paying customs and excise duties. In 1934, this business landed the Bronfman brothers and over a dozen other alleged co-conspirators of the so-called Montreal Group in the midst of a conspiracy trial. However, as outlined by Geof and Dorothy Robinson in *The Nellie J. Banks,* few convictions resulted.

It was alledged that a $5-million conspiracy ring existed and sixty-one people were charged in five provinces. Little came of the subsequent lengthy trial which commenced in January 1935. Charges against the Bronfmans were eventually thrown out by a Montreal judge who later became chairman of the Quebec Liquor Commission.

In the second so-called Halifax Organization, Riverport entrepreneur Willoughby Ritcey was identified as one of the principals. The role he played is sketched by the Robinsons in *It Came by the Boat Load* and *The Nellie J. Banks,* and by Jean Andrieux in *Over the Side* and *Rumrunners.* In due course, warrants were issued for over a dozen of the accused – among them W.R. – and the trials went ahead. A typical conviction – that of Howard Creaser of Riverport, one of several writs archived at the Fisheries Museum of the Atlantic – illustrates not only the extensive web of involvement throughout the Maritimes, but the remarkably light penalties eventually handed down.

According to record, Howard Creaser, together with William H. Awalt (Mahone Bay), Jack Creighton (Lower LaHave), Roy Ernst (Blockhouse), Thomas Fiander (Trinity, Newfoundland), George A. Mader (Mahone Bay), William S. Somers (Melford), and Clarence Tanner (Lunenburg) "did at Halifax in the County of Halifax and elsewhere between the first day of May, 1927, and the first day of February, 1936, unlawfully conspire together with one another and with" [Colin A. Chisholm, Bernard Cross, and Benjamin O. Johnson of Halifax; William Crawford (Berwick), Hugh McDougall (Hazel Hill), Frank Peturel (St. Pierre), and Willoughby Ritcey (Lower LaHave)], "and with divers other persons unknown to commit the following indictable offences."

In brief, Howard Creaser was convicted of the indictable offences of smuggling, possession, and selling "without lawful excuse, alcoholic liquor unlawfully imported into Canada, to wit, the provinces of Nova Scotia and Prince Edward Island, of a value for duty exceeding two hundred dollars whereon the duties lawfully payable had not been paid."

In the Supreme Court of Nova Scotia on March 24, 1936, J.L. Barnhill, Esquire, K.C., Stipendiary Magistrate, sentenced Creaser "to be imprisoned in the City Prison at Halifax ... for the term of one month and to forfeit and pay the sum of fifteen hundred dollars and also costs in the sum of three dollars, to be paid and applied according to law, and if the said sums were not paid to be imprisoned in the said City Prison and there to be kept for the space of three months."

Several other fellow conspirators, including locals Jack Creighton and Albert Eisenhauer, suffered a similar fate, although in money terms, it amounted to pretty small stuff considering the huge profits enjoyed by the organization. It almost seems that the authorities were acting to guard against killing the goose that laid the golden eggs.

Summing up, with respect to convictions among the Halifax-based conspirators, the Crown lawyer deemed it "competent to the Magistrate to amend the information by inserting after the words Halifax and elsewhere, to wit: LaHave in the County of Lunenburg and commit the accused accordingly."

The Crown Counsel concluded on March 24, 1936, that "The Bronfman case has no application," and that according to "The writer's recollection of that decision, legitimate sale of liquor in St. Pierre did not suffice to constitute a conspiracy to smuggle liquor into Canada, even though the liquor in question was ultimately smuggled into this country."

Jean Andrieux observes in *Over the Side* that "court action failed to halt the entrepreneurial instincts of the two Halifax members." Indeed, W.R. somehow managed to have his name scrubbed from the wanted list. However this was engineered, after Albert Eisenhauer reportedly took the rap for W.R., it was business as usual right on up to 1938. All things considered, both men will have had their own good reasons for viewing Albert's month-long stint in the slammer as time well wasted. It is said that Albert never again had any money worries. As for W.R.'s right-hand man, hearsay has it that Howie (Howard Creaser) was less than happy with the division of spoils resulting from the later sale of some ships – among them the *Muir, Standard Coaster,* and *Atacama* – which he and his partner jointly owned and operated.

According to John Gebhart in *The Last Outposts of Prohibition in Canada,* Riverport was the most important point on the rum-running map along the sixty-mile stretch of Lunenburg County seaboard from Riverport to Cape Sambro, near Halifax. With the repeal of Prohibition in 1933, the Banana Fleet ships were transferred to the Riverport Shipping Company, the Nova Scotia front for another American syndicate. Supply and demand, it seems, limited the operations of rum-runners more than any restrictions imposed by authorities. W.R., as it happened, had a firm hand in the Riverport Shipping Company, and the ships themselves remained under the watchful eye of Captain Byron Ritcey. *Marvita* and *Shulamite* were sold to the Newfoundland government whose intention it was to follow Hugh Corkum's example and use rum-runners to catch rum-runners. Others were tied up for years in Riverport and sold off one by one.

The star performer in the new fleet was the tanker *Standard Coaster*, purchased in 1936 by "the Nova Scotians" (according to *It Came by the Boat Load*) and captained by Norman Conrad. It seems that through direct dealing with the Black Diamond manufacturer in British Guiana, W.R. was able in 1935 to secure a monopoly on this prized dark rum, so favoured by Maritimers. A long-term deal was secured by the organization to have it shipped to St. Pierre in large puncheons, at which point it was repackaged for simpler delivery.

When the call came for captains for the new fleet, despite his recent misfortune, Winfred was still considered as one of the family. W.R. persuaded him to sign on. On August 31, 1934, Winfred was captain of the two-year old *Reo II*, owned by G.M. Morrell and Sydney C. Oland. W.R. owned several ships dedicated to rum-running, two of which – *Atacama* and *Maskinonque* or *Maskinonge*[1] – were among those reassigned to the Riverport Shipping Company following repeal of the Volstead Act. As a confidant of W.R., Winfred also served time as captain on each of these two vessels.

Atacama was a large motor vessel (115.2 feet long) built by Smith and Rhuland and registered on April 13, 1933. Especially constructed for W.R. and Howie in 1933, it was designed as a tanker in which several tanks were symmetrically arranged below deck.

1 Various spellings appear in the literature. Winfred's pronunciation of the name was close to the French maskelongé, meaning pike, unusual if only because it was considered unlucky to name a boat after a fish.

A powerful pump enabled the tanks to be filled or emptied very quickly, as required, the system being suitably ventilated. Like *Winona* and *Marvita* – two ships in the Banana Fleet – *Atacama* could deliver 10,000 gallons of Demerara following a return trip from the Caribbean. Winfred made several such business trips on *Atacama* on behalf of his employers, though very little is known about those adventures.

The *Standard Coaster* made up to five trips south for rum each year, a job previously performed by W.R.'s boats *Florran* and *Atacama*. A huge shore-based radio set, now on exhibit in the Fisheries Museum of the Atlantic, operated out of W.R.'s home in Lower LaHave during the rum-running era. Doubtless it played an important role in maintaining the communication so essential to smooth operations. According to the record in *The Captains of Lunenburg County*, Norman Conrad commanded several rum-runners including *Ada M., Standard Coaster, Ashtauria* [sic], and *Alpaca*.

During the mid-1930s, one of Winfred's main charges was the *Maskinonque*. Built by Shelburne Shipbuilding Ltd., at just over 92 feet long, it was a much smaller ship than *Atacama*. Much of the contraband, of course, found its way back to Upper Canada. Winfred's assignment was pretty straightforward – to deliver rum from St. Pierre to drop-off points or to contact boats, along the Maritime coast, including Cape Breton and the South Shore of Nova Scotia, both sides of the Fundy shore, and the eastern shore of New Brunswick. There can be no doubt that demand remained high, for as Rev. H.R. Grant bemoaned in a letter to the *Halifax Herald*, September 1, 1938 (without taking into account bootleg liquor), "the repeal of prohibitory legislation has been followed by increased consumption of liquor and consequent increase in crime."

As far as delivery of booze to Maritime communities was concerned, after it was set ashore, land couriers took care of things. Old folks in small-town Nova Scotia and along the eastern shore of New Brunswick recall with awe the large powerful cars used to take delivery following a shore drop. In New Brunswick, the preferred trade was mostly pure white alcohol known as Hand Brand and/or Star Brand in two-and-a-half-gallon tins. After Prohibition was lifted in the U.S., this could be obtained from a mother ship (the *Greta Kure*), which an enterprising St. Pierre merchant (Henri Moraze) conveniently anchored offshore beyond the territorial limit. Maritime rum-runners also were able to load up from regular supply ships from Europe. The greatest prosperity St. Pierre and Miquelon had ever known was coming to an end. France was concluding attractive new commercial treaties with the U.S. in response to pressure to end liquor shipments to the island. It was scarcely coincidence that the big money days of rum-running were running out.

While the good times lasted, Shediac, New Brunswick, could be counted as a very important port of call for rum-runners bringing booze. Most of it was destined for transport by road to Woodstock, where it was diluted for sale across the border. It's on record, for example, that *Alpaca* loaded up with 2,500 cases of spirits on November 11, 1935, from the Norwegian steamer *Reidun*, off St. Pierre, before heading northwest toward the east coast of New Brunswick. Ellen Lawson in *Smugglers, Bootleggers, and Scofflaws* includes a photograph of just such a transaction. Of course, the Canadian Preventive Service and the USCG knew all about such goings-on. Only one problem – the RCMP Patrol Boat *Argo* lost contact with *Alpaca* on that particular occasion due to dense fog.

For Winfred, Shediac and nearby Parlee Beach long remained favourite summer holiday haunts. Odds are that rum-running is what introduced him to that area's attractions. Then too, Parlee Beach is known for having the warmest saltwater swimming in Canada. Unlike most seamen of the time, Winfred was an accomplished swimmer. And he made no secret of the fact that he considered Parlee the next best thing to being in Bermuda.

Cross Island Calamities

"It has been known," explained the captain, "that when a bullet hits a keg it will run around inside and cause it to explode."

– Captain J.C. Kelly
to the coroner's jury in Lunenburg,
Halifax Herald, May 4, 1935

During the 1930s, operations were commonly mounted in the vicinity of Cross Island, about eight miles due east of Rose Bay, to transfer rum from mother ships to contact boats for runs along the South Shore of Nova Scotia. Most were accomplished without incident, although there were notable exceptions.

One case in point is described in Hugh Corkum's account *On Both Sides of the Law* when the RCMP cutter *Laurier* engaged his ship the *Marleton* southeast of Cross Island on July 25, 1937. During that encounter, *Laurier* fired 153 cannon shots and 250 rounds of small-calibre ammunition prior to seizing the rum-runner.

An incident two years earlier, though perhaps less spectacular, ended tragically on the night of May 2, 1935 when young Billy Tanner was gunned down by Captain J.C. "Machine Gun" Kelly of the RCMP cutter *Acadian*. The incident centred on a failed transfer of liquor from a mother ship – the 92-foot-long converted schooner

Muir owned by W.R.'s father, Captain Egerton Ritcey – to two contact boats about three miles southeast of Cross Island.

Despite the dark and the storm conditions at the time, *Muir* kept the rendezvous with the contact boats. The wind force registered seven (a small gale) on the Beaufort Scale, raising waves fifteen to twenty feet in height. There was no moon. But it seems that Captain John Courtney Kelly, an officer of the Customs and Excise Branch of the RCMP, was tipped off about the drop – more than likely thanks to a squealer somewhere in the works. Somehow, his small RCMP cutter *Acadian* made it to the rendezvous at about 10 p.m. just as the rum was being offloaded into the contact boats, according to Petty Officer Cooper aboard *Acadian*.

With a searchlight brought to bear on the alleged rum-runners, instead of concentrating on the motorship *Muir*, his professed target, Kelly was apparently distracted by what the *Halifax Herald* later described as a small, nameless motorboat, which took off toward Lunenburg Bay. During the race shoreward, a one-sided fusillade at sea about seven miles from Lunenburg northeast of Cross Island resulted in the death of William Tanner, a father of five from Eastern Points just offshore the mainland from Stonehurst.[1] The story goes, according to Kelly, that after his machine gun jammed, he used a high-powered rifle to try and explode a rum keg aboard the escaping craft. Meanwhile, *Muir* and the third boat escaped into the darkness. The identity of the third boat has never been satisfactorily established.

As for the boat on which Tanner met his death, Ted Hennigar in *The Rum Running Years* identifies it as the *Silver Arrow*. However, this is almost certainly incorrect because *Silver Arrow* was a regular rum-runner more than 100 feet long. More likely the boat was Willoughby's small (46-foot-long) Cape Islander, the *Silver Star II* out of Riverport. *Silver Star II* was a busy boat, doing business

---

1 The *Halifax Herald* of Saturday, May 4, 1935, relates this sea tragedy and details of the brief inquest which followed.

throughout the Maritimes. Shipping records show that Tanner served as captain of *Silver Star II* in November 1933. And in *I Was A Rum Runner,* Donald Miller tells about the seizure on October 14, 1932, of *Silver Star II* and her cargo of one hundred five-gallon kegs of rum near the coast of Grand Manan. In this instance, the alleged rum-runner got lucky: the charges were dropped, and the *Silver Star II* enjoyed the escort of a patrol vessel to the "wide freedom of the seas." Unfortunately, Tanner's luck did not hold. He was fifty-two years old at the time of his death.

During and after the inquiry, Kelly bore the brunt of criticism for his judgement call on the night of May 2, 1935, as well as for his backhanded apology for killing a man, when all he really meant to do, he said, was to ignite a keg of rum. Although the matter came up, Kelly was never indicted for murder. Indeed, no charges resulted from the coroner's inquest except for a $1,000 fine levelled against Tanner's companion on that fateful trip, Alton Mason.

William Aubrey Backman, a fellow captain and friend of Winfred's in the rum trade, relates that on the afternoon of May 3, when Kelly's boat pulled up to the Lunenburg wharf, Backman and six other men formed a line and told Kelly to get back in his boat and not return. Winfred was not among them. Subsequently, Kelly was posted to a district far removed from Lunenburg County. As for Winfred, it was only years later, as we fished one morning on the Shoal Ground – his favourite cod-fishing ground – some eight miles southeast of Cross Island that he let slip a comment that suggested he knew a good deal more than he was ready to admit about the third boat, and what took place on May 2, 1935.

I had asked Uncle Teddy more than once about the incident, for I knew he was familiar with the story. Were there any Maritime rum-runners who were not? He was not exactly forthcoming, although I was surprised to hear him refer to Cross Island as a "little rum row." He even ventured to add, "Quite a few drops were made along here, from mother ships lying just east of the island." Indeed, as confirmed by the *Herald* in July 1921, and again in the 1930s, there were numerous reports of mysterious boats landing booze at nearby Stonehurst before making clean getaways.

"So," I asked, "were you involved in those drops made off Cross Island years ago? How about that business with Machine Gun Kelly and the Tanner fellow from Blue Rocks?"

"Well, I might have been, in some of them. But that was a long time ago," Uncle Teddy replied, apparently having heard only the first part of my double-barrelled question. Knowing the man, this was as good as an admission. But I never did get a straight answer to the second part of the question. Much as he may have enjoyed a good sea story, he had his reasons not to encourage review of anyone's personal tragedy. These considerations aside, one got the message that he knew far more than he let on.

He certainly would have been alert to efforts by the RCMP to locate contraband hidden in the woods, along the shore, and in barns throughout Riverport and District. And while seizures were occasionally made, far more caches escaped detection by the authorities. Examples are not far to find. Marguerite Myra's Aunt Maggie, with but little prompting, could recount a rather comical case in point.

This centred on a police raid which failed to recover a cache hidden along the shore below her home opposite the Blue Sands (a.k.a. Sand Dollar Beach) in Upper Rose Bay because of its timely removal hours earlier by a party of local men. Apparently they had been alerted that the raid was about to be made. Aunt Maggie knew about such goings-on, of course, from past observations of unusual activities down by the shore, and she had a pretty good idea where the liquor was hidden. But she was busy that day spreading her potatoes and turnips on a tarpaulin to dry in the sun beside the house, before storing them in her cellar. And so, next morning was quite unable to assist the police when they questioned her about any unusual activities – even had she been willing to tell – for she was asleep when late that night the transfer was made from the shore cache onto her property. Neither she nor the RCMP realized the contraband lay safely hidden beneath the tarpaulin upon which her root crop was drying, there, in the morning sun.

Oxner's Beach in Lower LaHave was another popular drop-off point. One of the largest beaches in Lunenburg County, it served as a training ground for the militia during World War I. In Isaac de Razilly's day in the 1600s, it fronted an extensive pasture and salt marsh known as La Vacherie, where cattle brought over from France grazed contentedly. It seems that everyone heard about what happened to the cache buried at low tide beneath the sand of Oxner's Beach, the location foolishly marked by brush. All was in readiness for the owners to take delivery. Unfortunately, the recovery was not attempted until after high tide. It seems that somehow an act of God did away with the markers to the liquid treasure. Thus what ought to have been a simple straightforward transaction was foiled. Whether W.R. was the intended recipient of the drop is an interesting question. But in any case, pirates probably made the most of the situation.

It's virtually certain that Captain Winfred Spindler had a hand in some of those drops of contraband along this stretch of the South Shore. The schoolhouse heist described at the outset of this book was accomplished by a group of schoolchildren from the Lower Rose Bay School, less than a mile from Winfred's home. Perhaps the intended recipient was not at home at the time. Of course, that's all sheer speculation. It scarcely even qualifies as hearsay. Then again, the little rum row off Cross Island lies in plain view of Rose Bay, and smuggling activity post-1933 was relatively focused in those waters. Winfred knew them well, and so for that matter did Lloyd Heisler (as documented by Hennigar in *The Rum Running Years*), Nova Scotia's famous perennial International Senior Dory Rowing champion.

Winfred never rowed competitively, except perhaps against the clock in that ill-fated attempt to rescue his drowning friend, Calvin Lohnes from the *Ruby L. Pentz* back in October, 1920. In any case, he certainly knew better than to compete with Heisler in that arena.

On Heislers Island, now Rous Island, in Chester Bay, ca. 1960, two large men, Winfred Spindler, left, and Lloyd Heisler, make small talk, recalling old times.

But the two men knew each other well, and from time to time working from Cross Island both helped supply rum to customers in Riverport and District during the mid-1930s. There's no telling, but *Yahoo*, the small schooner in Winfred's charge late in 1934, may have played a part in those activities. Who would know for sure and certain at this late date?

Laura

Those eyes, 'neath which my passionate rapture rose,
The arms, hands, feet, the beauty that erewhile
Could my own soul from its own self beguile,
And in a separate world of dreams enclose,
The hair's bright tresses, full of golden glows,
And the soft lighting of the angelic smile
That changed this earth to some celestial isle,
Are now but dust, poor dust, that nothing knows.
And yet I live! Myself I grieve and scorn,
Left dark without the light I loved in vain,
Adrift in tempest on a bark forlorn;
Dead is the source of all my amorous strain,
Dry is the channel of my thoughts outworn,
And my sad harp can sound but notes of pain.

– Sonnet 292, one of many poems to Laura by Petrarch,
translated by Thomas Wentworth Higginson

To hear him tell it, Winfred's decision to marry came with the simple realization that he was not getting any younger. Sound familiar? The glory days of rum-running were fading from the scene nearly as fast as the ships themselves.

The Robinsons' *It Came by the Boat Load* documents the fate – in some cases quite colourful, in others simply unfortunate – of many rum-runner boats, including most of those in the Banana Fleet. Former commodore of the fleet, Captain Byron Ritcey, oversaw their maintenance and eventual sale under the aegis of the Riverport Shipping Company. Some were converted into freighters and went on to lead relatively famous lives. For example, *Kilmarnock* was converted by Admiral Byrd for work in Antarctica, and *Audrey B.* ended up working in the Arctic. Others, including *Eleanor B.* and *Reo II,* were used as target practice, much to the dismay of those locals who knew the souls of those ships more intimately.

Prior to her unceremonious execution fifty-seven kilometres northeast of Halifax at the explosive dumping range on February 24, 1985, *Reo II* enjoyed a chequered career under various captains, including Winfred. And despite the bullet holes that marked her hull and one porthole, she was a lucky ship. Built in Metegan in 1931 for the rum trade, she is said to have been the last rum-runner to operate off the American coast. As late as 1938, she is shown in an RCMP photo in the Robinsons' *Duty-Free* with a full cargo off Liverpool. Then, after serving as a coastal freighter from late 1938 to 1940, the navy requisitioned her for magnetic minesweeping. At war's end, she worked as a freighter in Newfoundland until retirement in 1965. Purchased in 1972 by the Fisheries Museum of the Atlantic, she became a star dockside exhibit in Lunenburg until 1984 when her deteriorating condition led to a calculated destruction. Winfred, for one, was greatly saddened to see her go.

Other boats, including the *Standard Coaster,* also saw war service. Except for a few sea trials, the *Titanic* of the fleet, the 175-foot-long *Jacqueline K.,* died of dry rot tied up in Riverport, never having carried a single load of contraband.

Atacama fulfilled her role as a tanker for W.R. and associates for about three years before her rum-running career ended. Shipping records show that in late July 1936, masquerading under the name *Jean Frances* (W.R.'s oldest daughter's name), she was ostensibly engaged on a mercy mission to Sable Island to rescue starving horses. More likely, it was a mercenary mission to pick up the horses for sale at auction in Halifax. Her captain on this exercise was Winfred's colleague, Aubrey Backman. According to the *Halifax Herald* (July 28, 1936), upon arrival in Kingsport in the Annapolis Valley, the famous ponies "appeared to be in good shape despite their sea voyage ... the majority have been sold ... Sorrell and Light Red predominate in the colour scheme of the ponies, which were on the whole fairly quiet ... it was originally planned to bring 100 ... but comfortable accommodation was limited." Early the following year, Winfred delivered *Atacama* to buyers in Panama. She was one of several stalwarts from the Banana Fleet that he delivered to Panama, making the return journey in the comparative luxury offered aboard passenger liners.

It's worth recalling at this point that Winfred earned his Master's Certificate in 1936 for a "steamship" not exceeding 150 tons. At the turn of the nineteenth century, under the Canada Shipping Act, all ships over 100 tons required the services of a captain who was certified to clear Customs for sailing to a foreign port. Unfortunately, most local captains, including Winfred, did not have a Foreign Trade certificate. However, the regulation was viewed as a mere technicality by shipowners, who simply registered their ships in the ninety-nine tonnage class, thus permitting the captain to clear his ship for the Foreign Trade.

Returning home from Panama via Havana to New York on the USS *Mongolia*, it's scarcely surprising that Winfred was impressed by the numerous deck chairs, built-in toilet facilities, church, swimming pools, and bars. He admitted to getting lost once or twice while exploring below decks on the great ship. According to his recollection, there were few chairs in a rum-runner. Small wonder he had fond memories of his cruises on luxury liners after years of being tossed about at the total whim of waves and weather in relatively tiny, albeit sturdy, banana-shaped rum-runners.

Like the rum-runner ships, their former captains also had to

Winfred Oswald Spindler and Laura Jane Veinotte married in Halifax on January 18, 1942.

switch jobs, a no-brainer for most men in this case. Winfred returned to shore fishing. He knew the business well, and it would allow him to remain close to home for a change. It was time to settle down. The timing was auspicious. As his teacher-sister Helen might well have reminded him, at forty-two he wasn't getting any younger, and "by the way, an attractive new teacher has been hired for the school in Upper Rose Bay." As if he didn't already know about Laura.

In those times, when book-learning was gradually beginning to be valued, teachers were considered an extremely fine catch. Winfred was well aware of this, and as a man of experience, he might not have required much encouragement. This enthusiasm would prove conspicuous by its absence in future matters of the heart – a testament no doubt of his first true love.

According to the marriage notice, the wedding took place (unattended) on Sunday, January 18, 1942, in Halifax, after which the couple "toured the province, and then returned to the groom's home at Rose Bay where they will reside." Laura was a twenty-seven-year-old Mahone Bay girl of Huguenot ancestry. In addition to good looks and professional skills, she was an accomplished seamstress. The young homemaker, one of whom any man would be proud, was a wonderfully welcome addition to "down home," as the Spindler household has always been known to family.

Winfred and Laura's first child, a boy, unfortunately died at birth, although the pregnancy went full term. The loss of their son inevitably took its traumatic toll. Then, to everyone's delight, on May 14, 1944, Laura gave birth in Bridgewater Hospital to a baby girl, Fay Elizabeth. In view of the extensive hemorrhaging Laura experienced, her doctor advised that she shouldn't have any more children.

Such advice was in those times not so easily followed. Laura conceived again. In a decision mirrored in the preference of many modern young women, she elected to have her child delivered in a private home by a midwife. Unfortunately, the medic's advice held true, and the young wife died from loss of blood on the day after the birth on February 28, 1947, of her third child, Freeman Veinotte.

During visitation held in the Lower Rose Bay homestead, according to custom, the blinds were drawn and the deceased was laid out in the parlour. As a nine-year-old, I was permitted by my grandmother to remain only a moment or two beside the casket because, in her words, I was too young. Even so, the experience made a lasting impression on me. The scent of formaldehyde was formidable. And I wondered about death. Mourners greeted each other in the adjacent kitchen, where a wood fire burned low. The rifle and double-barrelled shotgun hung guard over the entrance to the pantry and kitchen door respectively. They were fixtures. So, at this stage, was Winfred.

I shall never forget the scene as he opened the hallway door leading into the kitchen. Out in the hall was the telephone, fixed to the wall, where it remains to this day. The stairs beyond lead up to various cozy bedrooms and lovely sea views. Memories. All heads turned toward him. With both hands gripping the side of the door – totally inadequate as a crying post – he lurched like the drunken man he wasn't, through the doorway and into the kitchen. He did not cry, but his entire frame was the face of grief. He could not speak. After nodding acknowledgement to the sympathies offered, he staggered back again toward privacy.

In the hillside home of next-door neighbour Jean Corkum, his daughter, Fay, nearly three years old, fretted impatiently to go home.

"I want to go home. Look at all the cars and people. They're having fun. Why can't I go home and join the party? I want to have fun too."

They came from nearby, but unlike today, people lacked the luxury of coming from far away. The thinking was different then. The death of distance was still a decade or so away. My teenage sister Carolyn was in the midst of exams during her second year at Mount Allison University in Sackville, New Brunswick. My mother, in a Boston hospital at the time, advised her daughter by mail of Laura's death. Carolyn received the letter several days after the funeral.

It was over and done within a few days. Carolyn was exceedingly sad upon receiving the news. She was close to Laura. Upon completion of the academic year, she returned to Rose Bay and moved down home to look after Fay for several months. Eventually a housekeeper was hired. Life was becoming more complicated for Winfred, the family's breadwinner. His father John Solomon, crippled since falling from a hay wagon, required attention. And there was the question of his newborn son, Freeman Veinotte Spindler. He was named after John Solomon's older brother, Freeman Henry, lost by suicide at age thirty-five in 1902.

John Solomon, despite a jovial disposition, was a man familiar with grief and hard times, for he had lost all four siblings: brother Freeman Henry by suicide, and older teenage sister Ellen Susan, infant sister Alice Drusilla, and infant brother John (full name also John Solomon), all of diphtheria, one of several lethal plagues endemic in the community in those times. Considering family history, Winfred might well have concluded that Job's burden in life was scarcely something unique, but rather commonplace. Laura's passing was, so far as I am aware, never a subject for prolonged discussion within the family. Had it been brought up, elders' advice would have assigned the loss to God's will, and that would have been the end of it.

Matchmaking Soap Opera

By all means, marry. If you get a good wife, you'll become happy; if you get a bad one, you'll become a philosopher.

– Socrates (469-399 BCE)

Shortly after Freeman's birth, the family was fortunate to obtain a surrogate mother for the child. Through Winfred's sister Helen, Florence (Flossie) Romkey, a caring widow from Lower LaHave, was persuaded to take on the assignment. A dedicated Sunday school teacher, she had a reputation for taking good care of children, and her many talents included practical nursing experience. Her first husband, John Romkey, had passed away several years earlier[1]. So, for the next four years, a local maid was hired for housekeeping duties, while Winfred did his best to lose himself in the work of shore fishing. During this interval, with my father away at sea most of the time, and brother and sister away at college, I lived with my mother, known throughout the community as Helen Titus.[2]

Over time, Helen repeatedly relayed to Flossie her brother's

1 John Romkey lost his leg to blood poisoning while working on a schooner in Newfoundland.

2 Up until that time, local custom in this patriarchal society fairly dictated that wives were identified for routine purposes by their husband's first name.

willingness to commit to marriage with her. No secret was kept about this attempted matchmaking, for it was widely agreed this might help simplify matters all around, so I was bound to hear a good deal about it. This was during the late 1940s. But Flossie held out, remaining stoically indifferent to Mother's vicarious proposals. It seems Flossie had plans of her own. It was also no great secret that she was awaiting an offer from Irvin Himmelman of *his* hand in matrimony.

The net was therefore cast wider afield within Riverport and District. I've forgotten most of the inquiries made, but naturally enough there were bound to be several Ritceys. Madge Nauss would make a good match, I remember Mother telling me. As a schoolteacher and a socialite, she knew a lot of people. Mother shopped around while Madge presumably considered the proposal. But no, Madge declined. However, Miriam Ritcey, a strong, militant thirty-seven-year-old ex-Royal Canadian Air Force Sergeant Major from Riverport, accepted the challenge. During World War II she was with the RCAF Women's Division, having risen to Assistant Section Officer to serve at several training stations in Canada. Although her specialty was wireless, the badges she wore called for strong vocal cords. And like any good company sergeant major, she tested them regularly, for she stood for little nonsense.

Following marriage on August 29, 1951, in Trinity United Church, equilibrium was more or less restored down home. A year earlier Winfred's father, John Solomon, had passed away at eighty-one. Miriam, long accustomed to controlling her life, moved quickly to reunite the family, taking Freeman back from Flossie. However, disrupting any sort of familial tie – legal or not, real or imagined, or melded through practice – involves subjective factors. And Flossie was distressed by this. Freeman may have felt likewise.

John Ralph (Jack) was born to Miriam and Winfred on October 30, 1953. A delight to the family, Jack was a strong, cheerful child, showing great promise. In later years he would excel as an athlete and teacher of physical education. Even as a child he was

Winfred and his second wife, Miriam, in the Annapolis Valley, 1951.

fascinated by all things nautical, although this noble Maritime trait led in time, through plain bad luck, to tragic consequences. Freeman, a gentle soul some six years older than his brother, was prone in later years to sudden mood changes, which proved a fatal flaw in the last analysis. Suicide is not well suited to discussion. It is a subject better fitted to fiction.

The wheels of time grind on inexorably, driving the whirligig of family life. In 1965, Clara Augusta, grand old dowager and down-home mother-figure, passed away at age ninety-two, the last of her generation. Then, at fifty-seven, Miriam suffered a fatal aneurism on August 31, 1970. Flossie looked approvingly upon Freeman's marriage in 1972 to Patricia Meisner, a Lunenburg girl, hoping for the best for the child she so dearly loved. But it was not to be. Freeman's condition was not improved by shock treatment and the drug

Winfred and Flossie, his third wife, October 21, 1972.

choloropromizone, and in 1977, following discharge from the Nova Scotia Hospital in Dartmouth, he went for a long swim in Halifax harbour. Through it all Winfred, in enduring humility, courageously rolled with the punches delivered.

Winfred's older sister Helen, unremittingly persuasive as ever, gave Flossie little rest. It seemed that Irvin had not yet shown up to offer his hand. So it came about that, with a few extra nudges, Flossie gave in and married Winfred on October 21, 1972. As life's partner, she was pure gold, if one could dare think of such a match as an investment. Mistress of the art of generating good will, she was a totally caring soul whom everyone loved and respected. And she knew as much or more about rum-running as any woman who never sailed the seas. Her first husband, "lame Johnny," had been shore engineer with the Banana Fleet, the right-hand man of Captain Byron Ritcey, commodore of the fleet.

Flossie grew up in her ancestral home in Lower Kingsburg

on the shore front beside Hirtle's Beach. In the kitchen there, demon rum was as familiar a visitor as the booming sound of the surf, marking time on the shore. Keeping close company around the Enterprise stove, her father John Hirtle, her brother Paul, and her sister Gladys (of Gladee's Canteen fame) were all hopeless alcoholics. Her brother Cyril, developmentally challenged, was fortunately blessed with an unassailable good sense of humour and enduring pride in his ability to keep the family well supplied with firewood. Fortunately, he did not know enough – or more likely was not permitted – so far as I am aware, to make friends with the demon.[1]

Outnumbered, Flossie tried her best but could do little to control the situation. Cyril could only stand by and watch. That all members of the household survived that microcosmic rum war and lived to experience old age is a remarkable fact. Nearly as curious is the fact that Flossie, a physically unscathed veteran of that conflict, persevered through life in producing superb homemade wines of various sorts – rhubarb and dandelion especially – following her own recipes.

In her new home in Lower Rose Bay, she would venture a sip or two of wine on occasion with visitors. Gradually she got used to her new husband's preference for a glass of rum before dinner – to help his appetite, he said – though she was quick to whisk the bottle off the table and out of sight, lest visitors arrive and spot the incriminating evidence. Nor, if company were present, would she touch the rum bottle and glasses. She drew the line then and there. Winfred was ordered in no uncertain terms to "Get it yourself. I'll not touch the stuff." And so Winfred discovered that he was not totally helpless in his own kitchen, though he came very close.

---

1 One of Cyril's special talents was painting pumpkin figures chopping wood, out fishing, or rowing dories. Popular among tourists visiting Gladee's Canteen on Hirtle's Beach, his paintings commanded some fancy prices, enabling Cyril to more than pay his way in the Lower Kingsburg household.

Flashbacks

The make-and-break motorboat
Hauled high on the shore
Long since has gone totally rotten.
And those old fish shacks, they are no more,
Crumbled flat and nearly forgotten.

– Author unknown

In my young eyes Uncle Teddy always seemed an old-timer, familiar as fog, a constant reliable friend and yet somehow in a sense a stranger. Much like many parents, I suppose, for whom so much in life has already happened, and therefore a mystery in many respects from the perspective of a child. Snapshots supply glimpses of him as an ageless shore-fishing sea dog, and the life and times of the transitioning community in which he laboured.

For nearly forty years after rum-running, Winfred continued inshore fishing, much as his father before him. During the 1940s, his double-ender commonly made shore around noon, loaded to the gunnels with several quintals of cod. She carried a mast supporting mainsail and jib in those days, for Winfred loved sailing. With a fine pair of binoculars left over from Winfred's days as a rum-runner, Grandfather John Solomon and I watched from the down-home sun porch or veranda (depending on the weather) as he moored the double-ender in the middle of the harbour. Only then could he row his catch ashore. Unfortunately, the narrow shore frontage of the Spindler property was not blessed with deep water suitable for constructing a wharf. Inevitably, this translated to far more manhandling, lifting, and hauling than might otherwise have been the case. However, it cannot be said that Winfred's health suffered in any way, for he was rarely if ever sick.

Could be cod liver oil played an important role. After the shore work was done, every week or so he'd down a mouthful of oil from the barrel of cod livers kept just inside his fish shed. Doubtless the procedure would be condemned outright by any modern food inspection agency. Central to the ritual, initiated perhaps by his father, John Solomon, he used a wooden ladle kept specifically for the purpose to depress the floating layer of old livers, allowing the heavier oil to more or less fill the ladle. This went on all through the fishing season until the oil was sold in late fall for the manufacture of pills. I confess I lacked the courage to imitate my uncle, preferring instead a regular regime of cod liver oil tablets dispensed at home throughout the winter.

In the 1950s, when I fished with him regularly in the summers, the catches dropped off dramatically, thanks no doubt to the offshore international fleets of draggers. But if the profit margin changed, and it did, the excitement nevertheless remained. Fishing is like that. And in inshore fishing there is always something new to be seen. We would often hoist sail for the return trip, at least as far as Rose Head (Point), beyond which the wind generally drops off. Then, along the edge of the spruce-dark shore, even as we lowered the sails, deer occasionally appeared, unconcernedly munching upon wild peas, mustard, and bits of sun-dried kelp as if to tantalize my uncle, an avid hunter.

In the local lingo, my uncle just "played" at fishing in his later years. It was something to do. I sort of understood that, and took every opportunity to go along. The man was possessed of a thorough-going sort of country charisma. He was fun to be around. Just add in a fishing trip, and however trivial the catch, the exercise grew into an adventure. Bruce Mosher, his long-time deer-hunting companion, also often kept the old captain company out fishing. Winfred's boat never bore a name. Bruce had a much smaller one, and when he retired from fishing in 1976, he sold it to me. But that's another story.

A mile or so south of Cross Island used to be good ground for catching haddock, the preferred ingredient in fine fish chowder. A tossing bell buoy complains nearly non-stop about the relatively shallow water here and the foghorn from shore on the island moans unpredictably but all too often. Tides run like clockwork, no matter what the weather, and at other than slack water the current fairly rips along at this location. The best time for hand-lining is therefore at still-stand, the half-hour respite between tides. There's a regular parade of whales too, skulling along on secret missions to who knows where – the ends of the earth – sperm, sei, fin, humpback, and minke (according to activity recorded in the 1960s at the nearby whale-processing plant at Blandford, before Canada banned whale hunting in 1972). Despite the wars waged against them, a somewhat diminished parade continues today, according to the reports of whale watchers along the South Shore. Surprisingly, there are few entanglements of whales in nets set in Kingsburg Bay, although occasional strandings occur.

Winfred did not trust whales. He was afraid they might rise up from the depths and upset his boat, whether on purpose or not. "We really don't want a ride on a whale's back, do we?" he asked. I thought he was kidding, but in *Bluenose Skipper*, Gerald Gillespie confirms that Grand Banks dorymen on occasion were taken for unsolicited rides on Leviathan's back. Knowing this, Winfred, more than once while we were fishing, would up anchor and shift out of their path.

During herring season, every few days tuna would become trapped in the large herring seine net set by fishermen from Blue

Rocks, less than a mile north of the eastern tip of Rose Head. Blue sharks, porbeagle sharks, and dolphins abounded, as did the dogfish in their season, so abhorred by fishermen, especially those with nets to tend.

In Riverport and District, bootlegging provided gainful employment for small business enterprises in the community well into the 1950s and '60s. No less than eight bootleggers – all of them genuine Foreign Protestant stock – continued the tradition in Riverport during the 1950s. There's little harm in naming names here because, as the fellow said, "They're most of 'em all dead now anyway." Chief among them were Oscar Ritcey, Ronnie Kaizer, Randy Wentzell, Chester Wentzell (Randy's brother, a.k.a. Tchaikovsky), Pat Wentzell, and Lorne Romkey. Lennox Conrad, in his blacksmith shop across from Trinity United, although not really into bootlegging, always kept a supply of rum on hand for patrons. It's hard to say who was the most colourful of these unique characters, but my vote would be for Lorne Romkey.

Some folks might claim that Lorne (a.k.a. Al Capone) had never really had to work for a living since his deployment as a machine gunner during World War II. His parents owned Myrtle House, Riverport's only hotel. Despite the nickname, although an entrepreneur, this Al was not dangerous. On the contrary, he was generally well liked, and ever willing to help people. He had a hand in everything, including thoughtfully arranging dates for visiting fishermen with some local ladies, who from time to time took up temporary residence in a house near the school up the road from my home in Upper Rose Bay. Al also drove the local taxi, and managed a service station with a modest canteen. On Sunday mornings, he regularly held communion, opening his canteen at 10 a.m. sharp. Presiding over the party in his very own blind pig, the Prohibition term for an illegal bar, Al poured the good dark rum from a tea kettle at a dollar per shot. Funny thing, many church-going men at Trinity United seemed to prefer attending the evening service to the morning one.

A gallery of long-gone locals from Riverport. Left to right are Percy Himmelman, pianist and dairy farmer from Oxner's Side, East LaHave; Martin Wentzell, insurance salesman and shoe store owner; Paul Conrad, contractor; Irwin Himmelman, dairy farmer and brother to Percy; Pat (Earl) Wentzell (a.k.a. Eagle), bike shop owner, purveyor of guns and small arms ammunition. (Photograph by Gilbert Kempton)

Across the road from Lorne's Service Station, in his small bike and gun store, Pat Wentzell catered to younger clientele and gun owners like my uncle. He helped make ends meet by keeping a slot machine up and running in one corner. And for an extra fee, a generous dash of rum was supplied in his clients' soft drinks, to encourage the boys to play on. Pat liked music.

It was early September 1951, and school had not yet begun in earnest. The peak season for inshore hand-lining and net fishing was over. And although it is now scarcely politically correct to admit, Winfred, with the help of his flunky, regularly hunted grey seals in the fall, out beyond the bar at the harbour's entrance. Being a crack shot, and very handy with a long gaff, he experienced a fairly good success rate.

A dead seal tends to sink very soon after being fatally shot. Therefore, it was important to manoeuver the boat quickly over the spot where the kill was made, and to wield the gaff to good effect. In addition to helping spot the seals as they surfaced for air, my job was to manage the tiller and one-lunger (single cylinder) Acadia gas engine[1] – to start, to stop, or to trigger reverse on the switch in an instant – no simple assignment given such a temperamental beast of an engine. Through it all, time and again, I managed to dodge the fearsome flying flywheel on the thing without having my arm mangled. And at the end of the day, the government offered the magnificent bounty of ten dollars a snout. In those days, there were occasional barking packs of seals just out beyond the bar. Now, sad to relate, seals are almost as rare in Rose Bay as walrus on Sable Island. I wonder why.

When shorefishing, my uncle's unvaried breakfast routine consisted of tea, a slice or two of bread, and a couple of raw eggs. In a throwback to his rum-running days perhaps, he noisily emptied the eggs by suction, having first tapped tiny holes at the ends. My appetite is never keen at 4:30 a.m. in the morning. With eyes half-closed, I continued my waking dream about the luxury of a small Cape Island-style boat, complete with steering wheel (no flywheel), car engine (quiet, efficient), and cosy cabin (no cramped, anchor-fouled cuddy). But Uncle Teddy was old-fashioned, made of stern stuff, and would not likely change his ways. In later years, however, he had the mast removed – possibly to simplify things on board – and so sailing was no longer an option.

Doubtless there were some good reasons for his love of that old double-ender. They say that water can't put out the fire in the ignition system of a one-lunger. And nets can be hauled a whole lot easier at the bow of a double-ender than on a Cape Islander. There were certainly no bells or whistles on board, unless you count the battered tin foghorn stored behind the engine housing. It barely qualified as an alarm system, although on the rare occasions when

---

1 Acadia Gas Engine Company, manufacturer of these machines, was founded in 1908 by Winfred Theodore (W.T.) Ritcey of Riverport. In 1918, his company in Bridgewater peaked at over 100 workers.

the make and break failed to fire, it saved the old captain a lonely dark night on the water.

For whatever reason, none of the double-enders in Rose Bay bore a name. But each one sported a long wooden tiller providing direct drive to the rudder. On our way to do some hand-lining, at least in clear weather, the sight of the very tops of a cluster of masts on the horizon often served as our fish finder. An impressive reminder too, of our place in the big picture, mere specks bobbing about on a tiny wooden shell upon a mostly wet, closed, and rounded world.

A gallon earthenware crock held a (questionably) fresh water supply. And, known only to him and his sometime shipmates, a bottle of dark rum served as the sum total of what might qualify as medical supplies. Safely wrapped and cushioned, it kept company beside the water crock in the very stern of the boat. There were no life jackets. With the engine pounding away in reverse, and all controls at the stern of the boat, little help could be had were a man, working alone, to become entangled in rope or netting and pulled overboard while paying out at the bow. Setting a net in heavy weather calls for considerable agility, not to mention strength, even for a muscular acrobat rigged out in oilskins.

The process of cleaning and salting cod fish, as practised by shore fishermen back on dry land, was doubtless carried out more easily than upon the heaving deck of a salt-banker. Uncle Teddy was well used to both scenarios. It seems remarkable, but the entire rugged, unforgiving routine was duplicated on board Grand Bank schooners, even to the grindstone required for maintaining sharp knives used by throaters, headers, and splitters.

Uncle Teddy, it sometimes seemed to me, might have lacked certain handyman skills. He always invited help in sharpening his knives. He expected it to be done. For that function, Gabriel (Gabbie) Risser, a crippled old bachelor who lived alone near the Spindler homestead, did yeoman service as handyman. But I really suspect that my uncle faked his helplessness at times. He would trust neither my brother nor I to sharpen his splitting knife, the curved blade of which presented a particular challenge. Either he or Gabbie would do that job on a huge hand-operated grindstone. To any flunkies within call, however, fell the task of supplying the power. My uncle had a knack of making people feel important. But, after all, he was a captain, and captains could and did legitimately demand service from their men.

While shore fishing, Winfred had no need to resort to shooting the sun to find his position at sea. His seagull instinct always seemed to know, fog or no fog. Boxing the compass and the expert's touch of dead reckoning was second nature. If a course of southeast-by-east led straight to a good fishing ground or the red buoys of his first net marker, distance was the only other factor. That, and, of course, some allowance for the set of the tide, and perhaps the surprise of a lusty sneeze (for which he was well known) along the way. To the innocent, it would have seemed like magic. He knew the speed of his boat, he had a compass, and he had a pocket watch.

Winfred's favourite cod-fishing ground is known as Shoal Ground. You won't find it on any map but, trust me, it's there, a patch of flat, gravelly sea floor below about twenty fathoms of water some ten miles east-southeast of Rose Head. He could always find it, no matter the weather. My uncle, known as a very fine hand-liner, was happiest with two lines, one on either side of the boat, with a rubber nipper to protect each hand while guiding the lines. He knew by heart the water depths and sub-sea topography in Kingsburg Bay. Anchored on site, first thing was to run the lines off their wooden reels until the lead weights hit bottom. Then he would haul each back about two fathoms – twelve feet, give or take a few toes – his huge calloused hands reaching out in a body cross to effect the well-known measure. Immediately after securing the lines, the show began, baited hooks dancing either side, lifting and diving far below.

Winfred was never happier than when he was hauling large

Winfred in his double-ender, hand-lining for cod on Shoal Ground, in Kingsburg Bay.

cod fish on board. But one summer in the mid-1970s on Shoal Ground, he hooked a small halibut. The hundred-pound flat fish gave him more than the usual tussle. Dropping everything, he concentrated on bringing it to boat. For one man this can be quite a stunt, for quite apart from their ability to wreak havoc once on board, halibut have several tricks in their arsenal to evade capture. This fish will try and fool the fisherman into thinking that it has given up. It may rise toward the surface more quickly than the line is being hauled, which may lead the fisherman to believe that the gangen[1] has parted. Then, a sudden downward plunge snaps the line tight with a force which may exceed the strength of the line. Provided the fisherman passes this test, the slow and steady haul toward the surface is once more initiated. After several repeat performances of hauling and hoping, the fish may tire enough so that it

1 This name (for ganging) is given by South Shore fishermen to a strong and versatile moderate-weight hemp fishing line in widespread use at the time for fishing lines, binding on nets, etc. It is no longer readily available.

can be gaffed and/or clubbed into submission and somehow heaved into the boat.

This was an exciting business, and you never knew what would happen out fishing on any given day. Each trip was a fresh adventure. As flunky, I had little responsibility except to follow orders, even though this involved pretty well everything on board at one time or another, apart from the really heavy hauling. On this occasion the orders came thick and fast.

"Do you see him coming yet?" Looking down over the side of the boat, I spotted the flash of the big fish's white belly as it spiralled slowly upwards.

"Yes, here he comes."

"Stand by with the gaff!" And that too I had ready to hand, good flunky that I was.

Then, "Here, pass me the priest[1]!" he sang out, having at last wrestled the fish to the side of the boat, its head partly out of the water, one hand on the line, the other on a gaff fixed in the big fish's eye. I handed him the club, while with a nod of his head, he indicated the line saying, "Now hold this taut," at the same time making ready to deliver a couple of quick whacks on the halibut's head. Trembling, the fish allowed itself to be hauled on board by two very pleased and excited fishermen. For some time afterwards we were reminded of its presence on board by the rattling pen boards.

It was a good day's work except that we lost the anchor. It seems that at least one large obstacle – a glacial erratic perhaps – must have been left upon that otherwise gravelly patch of fishing ground. And it was on something like this that our anchor rope snagged. Backwards and forwards we maneuvered the boat, round and about, pulling and tugging, all to no avail. Finally, the rope parted.

About two weeks later, Winfred suggested we head out to

1 A stout wooden club used for subduing larger fish before hauling them on board.

Shoal Ground again to try our luck. I kidded him about maybe catching another halibut if he could find the same spot. It was a foggy morning, but there was lots of time left. We needed to get there well before eleven o'clock, by which time, breakfast for groundfish in Kingsburg Bay is generally over.

So, out came the box compass, and with an eye to the time, the course was set for Shoal Ground. After pounding our way through the fog for about an hour, we stopped and made anchor. "Well, here we are," Uncle Teddy declared, making ready his hand lines. Before long a few gulls dropped by to watch the proceedings while the gangen sawed away on the rail, back and forth with a steady hum, beckoning welcome tugs from below.

"Hello, what's this? I think I might have hooked one," he exclaimed as the line snapped tight in his hand. Then, "No, son of a gun, I think it's a snag. There, it's come free, but it's damn heavy whatever it is." Disappointment, succeeded by curiosity, was replaced by surprise, then astonishment when he realized that his hook was caught on a short length of rope, and that the rope was affixed to the very same anchor lost on our previous visit to Shoal Ground.

As a footnote to this flashback, Bruce Mosher, hunting and fishing companion of Winfred's, confided once that a short time after Winfred's son Freeman took his own life in 1977, Winfred remarked to him, "There are times I've considered doing the same." One day while out fishing, he even described to Bruce how simple it would be to do it: "It wouldn't be very difficult, you know, just a rope around your leg, and overboard with the anchor." Winfred, whose modest library contains a collection of books on seafaring and rum-running, likely knew the story of the rum-runner captain of the *Gloria P.H.* who, harassed by Machine Gun Kelly, met his death at sea, dragged to his doom not by Leviathan but by an anchor.[1] Winfred would also have known that his uncle, Freeman

1 As recounted in Janice Patton's *The Sinking of the I'm Alone.*

Henry, his son's namesake, had committed suicide seventy-five years earlier.

Having lost in succession his first-born son, two wives, and now his oldest son, Winfred's confession was fortunately recognized by Bruce as the warning sign it was. Relayed to family, Winfred's mental crisis was safely managed through counselling, averting further tragedy. But I have always wondered whether that chance recovery of his anchor on Shoal Ground had anything to do with my uncle's resolve to stay the course.

In truth, as life's hourglass ran out in his last decade, and despite relatively good health, Winfred would, in a weak moment, sometimes confess to having lost his *Eifer* – a well-worn term meaning zeal or enthusiasm, left over in Lunenburg County from one of the earliest Nova Scotian immigrant communities. He and his shipmates might well have pondered their *Eifer* during the winter run from St. Pierre to Rum Row, for at such times it was something you either had or you didn't. The giveaway to his state of mind was also evident in his oft-expressed impatience at the slow passage of time, so contrary to our common complaint of exactly the opposite. Yet in these same years, any friend or neighbour dropping in down home would find his welcoming face a visitation in hospitality. He'd enjoy a glass of rum and a cigar– preferably an Old Port which, according to the label, had been soaked in wine and dipped in rum – but all things considered, his life's compass was pretty well boxed.

His mother Clara Augusta, a former schoolteacher, saw to it that, whining or not, her young son made it over the hill to the nearby school for at least the first six or seven long years. By then the call of the sea was too strong, and his adventuresome spirit would be no longer denied. Neither can one can doubt the young man's experience in pursuit of the fairer sex, nor his merit as a soldier of sorts in the rum war. So much for the classic first four ages (infant, schoolboy, lover, and soldier) of man, according to Shakespeare. Nor was Winfred ever one to sit in judgement of others, much less to pass sentence. His preferred agenda drew heavily on discretion, and so his wise saws and modern examples were used sparingly throughout a long life. And he effectively dodged the sixth (slippered pantaloon) and seventh final age (second childhood), for he was never even close to senile. No canes or crutches for him. Caught in a time warp, his life simply wound down toward a lucid waking end. His tough constitution would only fall prey to a sober resignation of the will to live.

Crossing the Bar

For tho' from out our bourne of Time and Place
The flood may bear me far,
I hope to see my pilot face to face
When I have cros't the bar.

– "Crossing the Bar," Alfred, Lord Tennyson

The sea no longer provides much employment in small maritime communities like Riverport and District. Career seamen are scarce. Gone forever are the wooden vessels of the offshore fleet, shouldered aside by techno-savvy steel-hulled trawlers that relentlessly scour the banks along the Atlantic seaboard. Extinguished too, in the same breath – except for the religion of it all – the era of the great sea captains, their weather sense, navigational skills, and luck, eclipsed now by space-age circuit boards, pulsing glass screens, and lifeless white dials that speak.

One-time fishing villages like Riverport are slowly morphing into modest fair-weather retirement communities as families drift away. Yet the past is all around and the nearly forgotten lies close by underfoot. Along the waterfront and in the village, ghostly remnants from the rum-running days are scarcely perceptible. Unlike UNESCO World Heritage Site Lunenburg, where street-side tributes to the rum-running era abound, there are very few in Riverport. The slipstream of time has carried the place helplessly along with it. Nautical antiques can be had, of course, for a small consideration, an ancient sea chest perhaps, or a rusted anchor. And there by the side of the road in Lower LaHave, an eighteenth-century cannon hints of an even earlier vanished way of life.

The heydays of rum-running and fishing and fish-plant operations sustained by the entrepreneurial genius of founding families are consigned now to fading memory. Ox-blood red paint – an effective combination of cod liver oil and ox blood blended with lime wash – on buildings is, along with lobster factories, becoming a fast fading historical footnote. A few shore-fishing craft and several pleasure craft dot the waters of the LaHave estuary in high summer, but the big schooners are no more.

There is little left that suggests industry. Ritcey Brothers store, and the Ritcey and Creaser store, are no more. There is no longer a doctor in the entire district. And in the village of Riverport itself, there is no hotel, no service station, gun shop, barber shop, ice cream parlour, shoe store, bike shop, or grocery store. There remains one small working wharf and a post office, although closure of this latter threatens. The Customs Office disappeared years ago, likewise the telephone exchange. Three-quarters of a century after rum-running, the village is a shadow of its former self, struggling, like many companion communities elsewhere in the Maritimes, to survive, and sorely in need of reinvention. Despite successive cultural hits, hope is fed from stubborn, deep ancestral roots, and villages with souls somehow find ways to survive. There are encouraging signs.

The old Riverport School survives, though it no longer functions as such. It currently houses the Riverport and District Community Centre and the IOOF Confidence Lodge No. 106. Some justifiably view it as a small but significant focal point of local culture. In a sign of the times, perhaps, on the east side of the village the former Odd Fellows Hall has recently served as a venue and recording studio established by musician and producer Diego Medina. Recordings by well-known Maritime luminaries like Joel Plaskett and Matt Mays have been made here recently. There's no casino, pub, or theatre, no brewery, and as yet, no Doppelgänger of *Alpaca* or *Reo II* on show, but a renaissance of sorts may be edging into the picture. The Riverport Rum Runners Sea Festival, a highlight of which is a deep-sea fishing tournament, held at Kraut Point in early August, attracts a modest crowd of locals and visitors. And there have been wild rumours of establishing a rum distillery in the old school at Upper Rose Bay.

In plain view from Riverport across the river estuary is the LaHave Bakery and Market, and LaHave Outfitters which, catering to the needs of the sailing community, also hosts a small factory in which entrepreneur Jesse Watson manufactures skateboards for a modest global market. A recently launched schooner, *Tree of Life,* is moored beside the restored wharf. Rumours of bigger plans include a marina, chocolate factory, and a general store to supply the marine sector. In 2014, as Riverport celebrated its 250th anniversary, more than twenty Nova Scotian-built schooners arrived in the LaHave River estuary for the Nova Scotia Schooner Association's 52nd Annual Schooner Race Week. Looking on, Jesse's mother, Gael (who runs the LaHave Bakery), says that when she moved here in 1971, "I thought it was paradise. Still do."

Trinity United Church, in which Captain Winfred Oswald Spindler was long denied membership, struggles to survive the rapidly changing times. The patient care and craftsmanship manifest throughout the interior woodworking successfully challenges the fading exterior to do likewise and counter the ravages of time. Echoes of robust earlier days live on within the sanctuary. Even the pews in this church have memories, for they bear symbols of the sacred – carved as ship's wheels – to remind us of the sea, ever present and all-pervading in the lives and deaths in the community.

It was here that Winfred's passing was memorialized on Wednesday, February 24, 1993. Nothing like the mass meeting that convened one November evening sixty-nine years earlier to promote temperance and prohibition, instead a mostly sober gathering among which were represented many sons and daughters and grandchildren of former rum-runners. A collection of people assembled to honour the passing, after ninety-three years, of a simple fisherman whose homely charisma, good nature, and sea-won practical wisdom attracted the love and respect of those many friends and relations. Despite his preferred low profile within the community, he seems to have earned a certain local fame without ever having realized it.

Few among the gathering that afternoon in late February 1993 will have been consciously reminded of the days of rum-running. Yet there it was: the importance of the sea in people's lives; to the left of the tall organ pipes at the front of the church, in stained glass, a memorial to young Wesley L. Ritcey, snatched from life's promise at high noon on that dark day in mid-May 1933; and there, officiating in the pulpit, Winfred's minister, the Reverend Timothy Milley. Several months before his passing over (as Tennyson might have put it), my Uncle Teddy was brought up very short upon learning that his minister was none other than the grandson of Johnny Mossman, the Riverport Prohibition-Revenue Officer. Now what better champion could an incorrigible former rum-runner hope for to put in a good word or two for him as his life cycle comes full circle at the last trump?

Epilogue

Doubtless Tennyson would have approved of Winfred's request that his ashes be returned to the sea, acros't the bar at the entrance to Rose Bay harbour. The entire Spindler family was on board *Jana E.* that day in late February 1993, just off Rose Head, to see the patriarch's wish carried out. Winfred's son Jack was at the helm, and beside him his wife Beth, sons Brent and Ian, daughter Jana, his sister Fay, and her two girls, Lisa and Jackie. Taking turns, each in his or her own way paid tribute to the departed. Jana, then very young, said she remembered her grandfather making her laugh by dropping his teeth. Jack and Fay lit a cigar and had a few puffs in memory of their father as his mortal remains were swept away in a brief sparkling phosphorescent spray.

Winfred passed away on February 21, 1993. His third wife, Florence, outlived him by less than two years. It's just as well that he did not live to learn of the death of his youngest son Jack.

Everyone in the family died a little on October 20, 2001. That afternoon saw Captain Winfred (Junior) Risser and Jack Spindler – close childhood friends – along with two young deckhands on board Risser's Cape Islander crab boat, returning to port in Feltzen South. The *Ocean Sapphire* was heavily loaded with snow crab traps hauled from about fifty kilometres south of Lunenburg, it being

Jack Spindler

near the end of the season. A brand new lifeboat was in place on board. Jack, a member of the Coast Guard Auxiliary, had insisted on this, and he spared no trouble instructing the others in its use. After all, he was a teacher – the well-loved phys. ed. instructor at Berwick High School. Although a fisherman in his own right, fishing was now a weekend hobby, and Jack loved every minute of it. Much of his spare time was spent fishing out of Rose Bay on *Jana E.*, his own small Cape Islander. His father doubtless taught him all he knew about the sea, except for rum-running. But Jack thought in modern terms: no double-ender for him.

Everyone on board wondered at first when the *Ocean Sapphire* began settling quickly on the way in, initially at the stern, then at the bow. It was a fine sunny day, the wind moderate. Yet something was drastically wrong. Near Shoal Ground, the lifeboat launch was carried out smoothly, exactly as during a practice launch a few days earlier. And then, Jack took a short fatal step back on board, reportedly to retrieve life jackets for everyone. After that, it is not clear exactly what happened. Perhaps he wanted to make certain that their Mayday call went out. Accounts by local fishermen have *Ocean*

Sapphire going down by the bow, and the traps shifting forward blocking exit from the cabin, trapping Jack inside. The lifeboat's occupants looked on in horror. A tip became a plunge as the *Ocean Sapphire* was lost from sight. The stunned survivors were rescued several hours later by the Canadian patrol frigate HMCS *Toronto,* which was conducting exercises in the area.

A huge hole was left in the Spindler families. The consensus that a sprung-board caused the fatal leak did little to ease the trauma. Jack's name is the 711th carved in black granite on the Fisherman's Memorial on the Lunenburg waterfront. He was forty-seven years of age.

Acknowledgements

Special thanks to my publisher Lesley Choyce and to Pottersfield Press editors Julia Swan and Peggy Amirault for their splendid supporting role. Kate Kennedy and Andrea Mossman kindly provided constructive criticism of early drafts of the manuscript and called me back from several deadends.

My grateful thanks is extended to the following folks who helped this project to completion: Charlotte and Keith Boates, Linda Tolman, Gary Corkum, Captain Cecil Ritcey, Sheila Ritcey, Beth Spindler, Elroy Creaser, Gregg Ernst, Charlotte Corkum, John Wagner, John Kingwell, David Allen, John Kinley, Fay Aiken, Jean Mackenzie, Ronald Frampton, George Mossman, Carolyn Mossman, Norman Mossman, Maxwell Mosher, Subin Upadhyay, Gordon Stevens, Larry Risser, Irene Mosher, William Mosher, Maxwell Lohnes, Britanie Wentzell, Carol Hadjisterkoti, and Philip Hartling; to Kendra Power at the DesBrisay Museum, Bridgewater; to Lynne MacKay and Pierre Guevremont at the Blacksmith's Shop, Lunenburg; to Penny, Brogan, Alice, and Lisa at the Memorial Library, Wolfville, Nova Scotia; likewise Edward Williams and Nicolai Kasteljanov and Regina at the associated Public Internet Access Site; to Susan Abbott of the Textural Reference Section, National Archives, Washington, D.C.; and to Dwight Eisenhauer and Sueann Bailey of the Fisheries Museum of the Atlantic, Lunenburg, for courteous, competent advice. I am grateful to the Riverport and District Community Development Committee and especially to Jens Laursen for valuable advice on accessing photographic material, and in particular to Judy Allen, daughter of Phyllis and Cecil Ritcey, for permission to publish photographs taken by Gilbert Kempton. I am greatly indebted also to Dan Sweeney, Coordinator of the Printshop, Acadia University, Wolfville, Nova Scotia, for his expert technical assistance, and, last but not least, to Ralph Getson, former curator of the Fisheries Museum of the Atlantic, Lunenburg, Nova Scotia, for sustained unselfish donations of quality time and invaluable advice.

Appendix

There follows a list of the twenty ships, in approximate order of years, on which Winfred is known to have sailed up to 1938, giving the date, the ship's name, the captain's name, and Winfred's position on the ship.

1912 – *Revenue,* Captain John E. Zinck, Winfred sailed as flunky (quickly graduating to doryman)

1914 – *Lucille B. Creaser,* Captain Arthur (Enos Arthur) Creaser, doryman

Between 1912 and 1918 – *Harold Conrad,* Captain George E. Backman, deckhand

Between 1912 and 1918 – *Mona Marie,* Captain Lemuel J. Ritcey, doryman/deckhand

Between 1912 and 1918 – *Silver Arrow,* Captain Albert Himmelman, doryman

Between 1912 and 1918 – *Dorothy Earl,* Captain Charlie Donovan, (No record of this captain on this ship, though he captained *Alcala* in January 1925, and *Alpaca* in November 1932. His signature is on Winfred's certificate of discharge.) doryman

Between 1912 and 1918 – *Athena,* Captain Carl Himmelman (no record of this captain), doryman

1918 – *Frances W. Smith,* Captain Forman Mossman, doryman

ca. 1919 – *Progressive II,* Captain Carmen Knock, doryman

ca. 1920 – *Mary Pauline,* Captain Daniel H. Romkey, doryman

1920 – *Ruby L. Pentz,* Captain Calvin Joseph Lohnes, deckhand (racing)

1921 – *Annie B. Gerhardt,* Captain Robert Gerhardt, doryman

1922 – *Marjorie Hennigar,* Captain Byron D. Ritcey, mate

1923-1925 – *Alcala,* Captain John Roland (Roly) Knickle, mate

1927-1937 – *Alpaca,* captain

Date not established – *Josephine K.,* Captain William P. Cluett, position not known

1932-? – *Atacama,* Captain Fred Heckman (and Captain Winfred O. Spindler)

1934 (November) – *Yahoo,* captain

1934-? – *Maskinonque,* captain

1934 (August) and 1937 – *Reo II,* captain

Works Consulted

Allen, Everett, S., 1965. *The Black Ships: Runners of Prohibition*. Boston: Little Brown & Company.

Andrieux, Jean P., 1984. *Over the Side*. Lincoln, Ontario: W.F. Rannie.

Andrieux, Jean P., 1993. *Prohibition and St. Pierre*. Lincoln, Ontario: W.F. Rannie

Andrieux, Jean P., 2009. *Rumrunners*. St. John's, Newfoundland: Flanker Press.

Balcom, B.A., 1977. *History of the Lunenburg Fishing Industry*. Lunenburg, Nova Scotia: Lunenburg Marine Museum Society.

Barss, Peter, 1978. *Images of Lunenburg County*. Toronto: McClelland & Stewart.

Blocker, Jack S., Jr., Fahey, David M., and Tyrrell, Ian R., 2003. *Alcohol and Temperance in Modern History: an International Encyclopedia*. Santa Barbara: ABC-CLIO, Inc.

Bortner, Maude, ca. 1990. *Bits and Pieces of the Way it Was: Recollections of South and Rose Bay in the Early 1900s*. Unpublished papers.

Calder, J. William, 1977. *Booze and a Buck*. Antigonish, Nova Scotia: Formac Publishing Company.

Canney, Donald L., 1989. *Rum War: the U.S. Coast Guard and Prohibition*. Bicentennial Series, U.S. Coast Guard, Washington, D.C.

Carse, Robert, 1959. *Rum Row*. New York: Rinehart and Company.

Cherrington, Ernest H., 1921. *Anti-Saloon League Year Book*. Westerville, Ohio: Anti-Saloon League.

Cochrane, Jean, 1981. *The One-Room School in Canada*. Toronto: Fitzhenry and Whiteside.

Coffey, Thomas M., 1975. *The Long Thirst*. New York: W.W. Norton & Co.

Corbett, Scott, with Captain Manuel Zora, 1956. *The Sea Fox*. New York: Thomas Y. Crowell Company.

Corkum, Hugh H., 1989. *On Both Sides of the Law*. Hantsport, Nova Scotia: Lancelot Press.

Dawson, Joan, 1982. *Isaac de Razilly, 1587-1635: Founder of LaHave*. Lunenburg, Lunenburg Historical Society, LaHave, Nova Scotia.

De Charlevoix, Pierre François-Xavier, 1744. *Histoire et Description Générale de la Nouvelle-France*. Paris: chez Rolin Fils.

Forbes, Ernest, 1971. "Prohibition and the Social Gospel in Nova Scotia." *Acadiensis* vol. 2(1), Autumn p. 11-36.

Forbes, Ernest, 1988. "Rum in the Maritimes' Economy During the Prohibition Era." In Morrison and Moreira's *Tempered by Rum: Rum in the History of the Maritime Provinces*. Lawrencetown Beach, Nova Scotia: Pottersfield Press.

Francis, Daniel, 2014. *Closing Time: Prohibition, Rum Runners, and Border Wars*. Toronto: Douglas and McIntyre.

Furnas, Joseph C., 1965. *The Life and Times of The Late Demon Rum*. New York: G.P. Putnam's Sons.

Gebhart, John, Charles, 1929. *The Last Outposts of Prohibition in Canada: Nova Scotia and Prince Edward Island*. Washington. National Press Building, Washington, D.C. Association Against the Prohibition Amendment.

Geldert, Elwood, Charles, ca. 1967. *Farewell Old Salts* (two volumes). Unpublished.

Geldert, Elwood, Charles, ca. 1967. *Log, Lead, Lookouts*. Unpublished.

Gervais, Charles, Henry, and Gervais, Marty, 2009. *The Rumrunners: a Prohibition Scrapbook*. 30th Anniversary Edition. Thornhill, Ontario: Biblioasis.

Gillespie, G.J., 1955. *Bluenose Skipper*. Fredericton, New Brunswick: Brunswick Press.

Grant, Barry J., 1984. *When Rum Was King: The Story of the Prohibition Era in New Brunswick*. Fredericton, New Brunswick: Fiddlehead Poetry Books.

Guildford, Janet, and Morton, Susan, 1993. *Separate Spheres: Women's Worlds in the 19th-Century Maritimes*. Fredericton, New Brunswick: Acadiensis Press.

Hennigar, Ted R., 1981. *The Rum Running Years.* Hantsport, Nova Scotia: Lancelot Press.

Hunt, C.W., 1988. *Booze, Boats and Billions.* Toronto: McClelland & Stewart.

Lawlor, Allison, 2009. *Rum-Running.* Halifax, Nova Scotia: Nimbus Publishing Ltd.

Lawson, Ellen Nickerson, 2013. *Smugglers, Bootleggers, and Scofflaws.* Albany, New York: Excelsior Editions.

Leach, MacEdward, 1965. *Folk Ballads and Songs of the Lower Labrador Coast.* Ottawa. Bulletin No. 201, Anthropological series No. 68. National Museum of Canada.

Leefe, John, 1999. *The Atlantic Privateers.* Liverpool, Nova Scotia. The Canadian Studies Foundation.

Lohnes, Maxwell, ca. 2008. *Captains of Lunenburg County.* Lunenburg, Nova Scotia: Fisheries Museum of the Atlantic. Unpublished.

MacMechan, Archibald. 2011. *In the Great Days of Sail* (Edited by Elizabeth Peirce). Halifax, Nova Scotia: Nimbus Publishing.

McKenna, Lloyd C., 2011. *Atlantic Canadian Rum Runners.* Charlottetown, Pince Edward Island (self-published).

Miller, Donald, 1979. *I was a Rum Runner.* Yarmouth, Nova Scotia: Lescarbot Printing Ltd. (self-published).

Moreira, James, 1965. *A Burning Mercy: Rum in the Atlantic Provinces.* Catalogue of the Federation of Nova Scotian Heritage, Halifax.

Morrison, James H., and Moreira, James (editors), 1988. *Tempered by Rum: Rum in the History of the Maritime Provinces.* Lawrencetown Beach, Nova Scotia: Pottersfield Press.

Nelson, Derek, 1995. *Moonshiners, Bootleggers and Rumrunners.* Osceola, Wisconsin: Motorbooks International Publishers and Wholesalers.

Parker, John P., 1996. *Sails of the Maritimes.* Toronto: McGraw-Hill Ryerson Ltd.

Parker, Michael, 1999. *Images of our Past – Historic Lunenburg – The Days of Sail.* Halifax, Nova Scotia: Nimbus Publishing.

Patton, Janice, 1973. *The Sinking of the I'm Alone.* Toronto: McClelland & Stewart Ltd.

Randell, Jack, 1930. *I'm Alone.* Brooklyn, New York: Bobbs-Merrill Co.

Ricci, Joseph A., 2011. *All Necessary Force: The Coast Guard and the Sinking of the I'm Alone.* M.A. Thesis 1342, University of New Orleans.

Robinson, Geoffrey and Dorothy, 1970. *The Nellie J. Banks.* Summmerside, Prince Edward Island (self-published).

Robinson, Geoffrey and Dorothy, 1983. *It Came by the Boat Load.* Summerside, Prince Edward Island (self-published).

Robinson, Geoffrey and Dorothy, 1992. *Duty-Free: A Prohibition Special.* Summerside, Prince Edward Island (self-published).

Robert, Lewis Taylor, 1966. *Vessel of Wrath: the Life and Times of Carry Nation.* New York: The New American Library.

Rose, Clifford, 1980. *Four Years with the Demon Rum.* Fredericton, New Brunswick: Acadiensis Press.

Smith, Captain Frank C., ca 1975. *Marine History of the LaHave River.* Lunenburg, Nova Scotia. Unpublished document prepared for the Fisheries Museum of the Atlantic.

Standage, Tom, 2005. *A History of the World in Six Glasses.* Walker & Co.

Sutton, Eddy, 1995. *A Little Booze Story.* Yarmouth, Nova Scotia: E. Sutton Enterprises (self-published).

Taylor M. Brook, 2006. *A Camera on the Banks: Frederick William Wallace and the Fishermen of Nova Scotia.* Fredericton, New Brunswick: Goose Lane Editions.

Willoughby, Malcolm, F., 1964. *Rum War at Sea.* Washington, D.C.: Government Printing Office.